MAKERS OF
MODERN CHRISTIAN
SOCIAL THOUGHT

LEO XIII AND ABRAHAM KUYPER
ON THE SOCIAL QUESTION

MAKERS OF
MODERN CHRISTIAN
SOCIAL THOUGHT

LEO XIII AND ABRAHAM KUYPER
ON THE SOCIAL QUESTION

EDITED BY JORDAN J. BALLOR

ACTONINSTITUTE

ISBN 978-1-942503-45-3

On the cover: Workers' Demonstration, Paris (c. 1900), by frères Seeberger. Rijksmuseum. Public domain. / Portrait of Pope Leo XIII (c. 1898). Wikimedia Commons. Public domain. / Photograph of Abraham Kuyper from W. E. Griffis' *The American in Holland* (1899). Wikimedia Commons. Public domain.

ACTONINSTITUTE

98 E. Fulton
Grand Rapids, Michigan 49503
Phone: 616.454.3080
Fax: 616.454.9454
www.acton.org

Interior composition: Judy Schafer
Cover: Scaturro Design

Printed in the United States of America

Contents

INTRODUCTION

Introduction

Leo XIII, Abraham Kuyper, and the Foundations of Modern Christian Social Thought

JORDAN J. BALLOR

"When a society is perishing," wrote Pope Leo XIII in 1891, "the wholesome advice to give to those who would restore it is to call it to the principles from which it sprang."[1] These words are as true today as they were when first written 125 years ago, and in our own time of social upheaval, insecurity, and anxiety we ought to take Leo's guidance to heart. To aid recall of the principles upon which Christian social reflection has been founded in the modern age, this volume contains the text of Leo XIII's encyclical on the relationship between labor and capital and Abraham Kuyper's speech to the first Christian Social Congress in Amsterdam. These two works, both published in 1891, should rightly be understood as foundational sources for subsequent Christian social thought in their respective traditions—Roman Catholic and Reformed.[2] Although many of the particular circumstances and the dynamics at play are different today than they were more than a century ago, the thought of these two theologians—one an Italian scholar-pope and the other a Dutch Reformed pastor, professor, and politician—provide enduring wisdom for developing and articulating a Christian witness in the modern world.

Background and Context

Europe in the nineteenth century is often depicted as a place of optimism and progress. Revolutions of various kinds had swept through or were in the process of sweeping across the continent, and progress, whether political, economic, moral, or intellectual, was the promised result. If hope dawned in the early decades of the century, by its close dark clouds had formed and cast a shadow across the continent. The political revolutions of the eighteenth century in Europe and America had unleashed forces of democratization, industrialization, urbanization, and rationalization. These forces brought enormous benefits, but also sometimes resulted in upheaval and conflict. While America experienced a bloody war between North and South, Europe was convulsed by social instability and increasing dissatisfaction with the pace of revolutionary progress.

Gross domestic product (GDP) per capita in Germany more than tripled from the beginning to the end of the nineteenth century. Over that same period, per capita GDP had doubled in the United Kingdom, while in France, GDP per capita nearly doubled between 1850 and 1900.[3] Economic growth, by at least this measure, was a reality in nineteenth-century Europe. Yet with economic growth came significant social challenges. Increasing industrialization and innovation powered developing economies and created significant growth, but also created new, troubling dynamics between workers, management, and owners. While per capita GDP was growing by leaps and bounds through the century in Europe, so too were the populations of these nations. In 1800, Europe had roughly 187 million inhabitants. A century later, there were more than 400 million people living there.[4] Such rapid population growth created further pressures on existing government and private institutions.

Social reformers and revolutionaries organized movements and campaigns across the continent to respond to the shifting economic and political realities. The two dominant approaches to these issues can be broadly identified as liberal and collectivist. The former approach emphasizes the rights of the individual human being over against powers inherent in social institutions, particularly the government. The latter approach subsumes individuals within claims of obedience and loyalty to a larger community. In the nineteenth century both views tended to take the nation-state as a point of departure for revolution and reform. While these two perspectives are often understood as embodying contrary impulses, in reality they are more like ends of a spectrum, with a wide diversity of social movements coming to particularized expression in different nations and from different ideological and confessional commitments.[5] Leo XIII clearly identifies socialism, a family of collectivist social philosophies, as one of the preeminent dangers to the social order at the close of the century, and for good reason. Popular uprisings are fomented by glaring inequalities of wealth and power, and revolutionary doctrines present the real possibility of civil unrest. Leo's encyclical is thus aimed at a world wracked by angst and uncertainty, and where collectivist socialism presents an immediate revolutionary threat. "Socialists," says Leo, "working on the poor man's envy of the rich, are striving to do away with private property, and contend that individual possessions should become the common property of all, to be administered by the State or by municipal bodies."[6] The actualization of such a program would be disastrous. Thus Leo warns of the socialists: "that ideal equality about which they entertain pleasant dreams would be in reality the levelling down of all to a like condition of misery and degradation."[7]

While Leo's letter casts a pan-European vision, Kuyper's address is more specifically focused on his domestic context. Industrial development arrived relatively late to the Netherlands, a nation characterized by difficult terrain and formidable infrastructure challenges. Leo's encyclical was promulgated in the early summer of 1891 while momentum for a social congress, a gathering of representatives and leaders from a variety of Christian institutions and churches, was rapidly mounting. Abraham Kuyper, who had led the exodus of a group from the established church in the Netherlands two years before, was mired in ecclesiastical and civil political maneuvering.[8] The first Christian Social Congress in Amsterdam was held on November 9–12, 1891, and was intended to form a Reformed consensus on a way through growing conflicts between labor and ownership, lower and upper classes, and visions of church and social leadership.[9] Although distinctive in their own ways, Leo and Kuyper's reflections on Christianity and its relevance for the social question illustrate remarkable commonality and coherence on a variety of foundational points, including the centrality of the doctrine of anthropology, the significance of private property and human stewardship, and the normative value of the principles of subsidiarity and solidarity.

The Human Person and the Social Question

For his part, Abraham Kuyper identified a key conceptual and genetic link between a kind of atomistic individualism and collectivistic socialism.[10] Liberal theory for Kuyper was most identifiable with the spirit of the French Revolution, which attempted to sever the bonds between the past and the present, between the classes, and between religion and public life. The sovereign individual was lifted up as the ideal of enlightened humanity. In connection with this picture of the human person, however, there arose theories of social and political order that emphasized the state and central political authority as the driving force for human progress.

One of Kuyper's key criticisms of these dominant ideologies was to identify them as reverse images of one another. Thus, he contends, "It is not enough to say that the social-democratic movement issues from the liberal theory. It must also be stressed that the liberal calls for a totally arbitrary halt on a trajectory that according to his theory has to be followed. Thus the liberal has spiritual kinship with the social democrat, but unlike him he is in the wrong, because he is arbitrary, self-serving, and inconsistent."[11] When the sovereign individual has been liberated from all social bonds and social authorities other than those that are voluntarily entered into by means of contract, institutions like family, church, and other associations of civil society fade into obscurity. All that is left is the individual and the state, which serves as the nexus of identity and the enforcer of social progress.

Leo XIII likewise recognized the dangers in politicizing all social relationships and obligations. In the case of the church and duties of Christian charity, for instance, Leo affirms the priority of what we might call civil society. Thus, he writes, "At the present day many there are who, like the heathen of old, seek to blame and condemn the Church for such eminent charity. They would substitute in its stead a system of relief organized by the State. But no human expedients will ever make up for the devotedness and self-sacrifice of Christian charity."[12] Against the twin errors of radical individualism and totalitarian collectivism, Leo asserts the rights of persons and institutions, such as the family and the church, for a flourishing social order. "We have said that the State must not absorb the individual or the family; both should be allowed free and untrammelled action so far as is consistent with the common good and the interest of others," he concludes.[13]

These criticisms of both atomistic individualism and collectivistic socialism turn on the Christian vision of the human person created in God's image for communion with him and community with one another.[14] Kuyper writes that "the Christian religion seeks the dignity of the human person in the relationships of an organically integrated society."[15] A Christian approach to the social question depends on a proper understanding of the human person, respect for civil society, and realistic and sober appreciation for the role of government. If the social question is cast in terms of the relationships of capital and labor, an authentic Christian response requires a comprehensive understanding of the human person and social order. This means, in the first place, appreciation of the dignity of the human person and the rich diversity of social institutions. "There will ever be differences and inequalities of condition in the State," writes Leo. "Society cannot exist or be conceived of without them."[16] Where Kuyper speaks of the organic unity of society, Leo emphasizes the mutuality of social relationships. Thus, writes Leo, "The great mistake made in regard to the matter now under consideration is to take up with the notion that class is naturally hostile to class, and that the wealthy and the working men are intended by nature to live in mutual conflict." In fact, he concludes, "Each needs the other: capital cannot do without labor, nor labor without capital."[17]

Property and Stewardship

A Christian vision of the human person does not make ultimate distinctions based on class or other social constructs. There is a foundation of dignity and formal equality that must be respected within the context of the diversity of dispositions, gifts, talents, and responsibilities. For Leo, a key aspect to the solution of the relationship between labor and capital lies in respecting the property rights of everyone, rich or poor, owners and workers alike. "The first and most fundamental principle, therefore, if one would undertake to alleviate the condition of the masses, must be the inviolability of private property," writes Leo.[18] The major threat to private property from the side of the socialists is government expropriation of the fruits of labor along with the reserves of capital. Against the socialization of property the pope asserts the prior rights of human beings to work and live from the produce of that work: "Man precedes the State, and possesses, prior to the formation of any State, the right of providing for the substance of his body."[19]

If the derogation of property rights is a hallmark of the socialist error, the absolutization of property rights is characteristic of liberal, individualist theory. The Christian vision of property and the human person similarly opposes this latter mistake.[20] Thus Leo distinguishes between the right to own property and the right to dispose of it in any way: "it is one thing to have a right to the possession of money and another to have a right to use money as one wills."[21] This distinction shows how stewardship responsibilities attend to property rights.

Kuyper opens his positive vision of the social question by asserting the foundational reality of human work and responsibility. Thus, he writes, "Our human nature is placed in the nature that surrounds us, not in order to leave nature as it is, but to work on nature instinctively and irrepressibly, by means of art, to improve and perfect it."[22] The fruit of this cultivating work is property as well as cultural development and technological progress. This work is oriented not primarily to self-aggrandizement or the satiation of selfish desires, but is rather to be focused on the service of others in obedience to God's commandment.

In this way Kuyper strongly asserts the responsibilities of positive stewardship that go along with all of the gifts God has distributed throughout creation. The Christian, says Kuyper, "has to bear witness that there can be no question of absolute ownership except in the case of God himself, and that all our possessions are only held on loan from him. We manage our possessions only as a form of stewardship."[23] The consequence of this is twofold. First, there is a clear responsibility to put these gifts into productive service: "none but God the Lord can release us from our responsibility for managing those possessions." Second, there is a social, other-directed orientation of that management: "we can never have any other property right than in association with the organic coherence of mankind, hence also with the organic coherence of mankind's goods."[24] Leo likewise connects the fundamental rights to property to the clear moral obligations to employ that property in the service of others: "Whoever has received from the divine bounty a large share of temporal blessings, whether they be external and material, or gifts of the mind, has received them for the purpose of using them for the perfecting of his own nature, and, at the same time, that he may employ them, as the steward of God's providence, for the benefit of others."[25]

Subsidiarity and Sphere Sovereignty

As each person enjoys a particular stewardship responsibility arising out of a particular set of talents, gifts, relationships, and property, formulation of a social principle respecting that diversity is required. The ideas laid out in *Rerum Novarum* on this theme would later be more formally articulated as the principle of subsidiarity. The classic statement of this principle appears in the encyclical *Quadragesimo Anno* of Pope Pius XI, promulgated in 1931 on the fortieth anniversary of *Rerum Novarum*. As Pius writes, "Just as it is gravely wrong to take from individuals what they can accomplish by their own initiative and industry and give it to the community, so also is it an injustice and at the same time a grave evil and disturbance of right order to assign to a greater and higher association what lesser and subordinate organizations can do. For every social activity ought of its very nature to furnish help to the members of the body social, and never destroy and absorb them."[26]

In this way subsidiarity is a principle aimed at respecting social diversity. As Leo writes, "There naturally exist among mankind manifold differences of the most important kind; people differ in capacity, skill, health, strength; and unequal fortune is a necessary result of unequal condition." This inequality is not necessarily damaging or the result of sin. In fact, avers Leo, "Such unequality is far from being disadvantageous either to individuals or to the community. Social and public life can only be maintained by means of various kinds of capacity for business and the playing of many parts; and each man, as a rule, chooses the part which suits his own peculiar domestic condition."[27]

The corresponding concept in Kuyper's thought, aimed at respecting and reflecting the rich variety of institutional and vocational commitments in social life, is the principle of sphere sovereignty. Kuyper had previously articulated this principle in his defense of the foundation of a new educational institution, free of direct control by either church or state. Whereas the modern Roman Catholic articulations of subsidiarity tend to emphasize a hierarchy of social institutions (Pius' "greater and higher" associations and "lesser and subordinate organizations"), Kuyper's principle of sphere sovereignty is a distinctively Reformed version of the principle that emphasizes the formal equality of all social spheres and institutions before God. "Our human life, with its visible material foreground and invisible spiritual background, is neither simple nor uniform but constitutes an infinitely complex organism," asserts Kuyper. And the complexity of social life must be respected through an understanding of the sovereignty of these institutions derived from and authorized by Christ: "Human freedom is safe under this Son of Man anointed as Sovereign because, along with the State, every other sphere of life recognizes an authority derived from Him—that is, possesses sovereignty in its own sphere."[28]

These versions of subsidiarity, while not identical, are best understood as embodying different, and perhaps even complementary, emphases. One is more hierarchical and top-down, while the other is more egalitarian and bottom-up. Both, however, are intended to reflect and respect the rich diversity of social life and the institutional expressions of human sociality. In the context of the social question at the end of the nineteenth century, this principle of diversity came to particular expression in concerns about the legitimacy and scope of state intervention in social relationships, whether that of the family or the workplace. Both Kuyper and Leo allow for the validity of state action into the life of the different spheres, but clearly limit such action to a function of temporary intervention with the aim of revitalizing and restoring corrupted and malfunctioning institutions.[29] To accord with subsidiarity, such state action cannot be a permanent or unconditioned feature of social life.

Solidarity and Sphere Universality

If subsidiarity and sphere sovereignty respect social diversity, the principles of solidarity and sphere universality respond to the realities of social unity. State action will often be necessary to alleviate suffering, for instance, precisely because each person is created in the image of God and there is a shared identity and bond that connects all human beings to one another. As Leo writes, "If Christian precepts prevail, the respective classes will not only be united in the bonds of friendship, but also in those of brotherly love."[30] Pope John Paul II later explicates the moral responsibilities arising out of solidarity in connection with the family and working outward from this primary institution of love.[31]

Kuyper's concern for the poor is a remarkable feature of his address as well as a number of his other writings. Here Kuyper indicts Christians who are complacent about the plight of the poor: "But there is no excuse for a situation in which our heavenly Father with divine generosity causes an abundance of food to come forth from the ground and that through our fault this bounty is distributed so unequally that while one person has more than enough to eat the other goes to bed with an empty stomach—if he even has a bed."[32] In the midst of Kuyper's concern that the social question be addressed seriously and soberly, he likewise emphasizes the necessity of action. Thus, he writes, "*actions*, acts of love, are also crucial. Obviously, the poor man cannot wait until the restoration of our social structure has been completed."[33]

Less well-known than the concept of sphere sovereignty is the corresponding concept of sphere universality. These spheres are not absolutely isolated and unrelated aspects of social order. They must relate positively to one another and be united in an orientation toward human flourishing. The unity that the concept points to is not simply a temporal unity, however. It is oriented toward the eternal unity of human persons in relationship with others and with God.[34] In this way sphere universality accords with solidarity and the common good since they are rooted in God's transcendence.

For Leo, the grounding of temporal existence in eternity is likewise necessary: "The things of earth cannot be understood or valued aright without taking into consideration the life to come, the life that will know no death. Exclude the idea of futurity, and forthwith the very notion of what is good and right would perish; nay, the whole scheme of the universe would become a dark and unfathomable mystery."[35] Thus solidarity also connects with the Roman Catholic idea of the universal destination of goods. As Pope Paul VI would write in his encyclical letter *Populorum Progressio*, "No one may appropriate surplus goods solely for his own private use when others lack the bare necessities of life."[36] This obligation is grounded in the idea that the earth is itself intended for common use and the common benefit of all. Leo XIII connects this idea with the natural right to work: "It necessarily follows that each one has a natural right to procure what is required in order to live, and the poor can procure that in no other way than by what they can earn through their work."[37] In this way, the right to private property for everyone is related to the common right to work and provide for oneself and one's family. This right, in turn, is grounded in the divine provision of the earth as the source of common bounty for all.

Solidarity and subsidiarity are rightly understood as necessary complements. They can be used as principles for understanding whether the realities of diversity and unity are being respected and acknowledged. For instance, when another institution helps a family that is suffering material deprivation, this help can be understood as an expression of true subsidiarity only if the needs are met in such a way that people are not driven apart and community is not fragmented. In order for it to be genuinely helpful, it must heal and sustain community. The goal for such intervention must be to restore the proper functioning of the ailing community, thereby supporting its continued existence. Help must thus be offered as a response to the reality of solidarity, but in a way that respects institutional sovereignty and diversity. Thus, assistance arising from the motive of solidarity and unity must be offered in a way that affirms and upholds the dignity and diversity of social life in accord with subsidiarity.

Conclusion: 125 Years and Beyond

Abraham Kuyper's "The Social Question and the Christian Religion" and Leo XIII's *Rerum Novarum* inaugurated more than a century of sustained modern Christian social thought. In the case of the Christian Social Congress, the formal, institutional setting for such reflection did not endure as it has in the case of the Roman Catholic Church.[38] By its very nature Protestant social teaching, to the extent that it is a coherent body of doctrine, is more diffuse and diverse, reflecting the institutional and ecclesial diversity of Protestantism itself. While there were subsequent social congresses and conferences in the Netherlands and Europe, other bodies, including ecumenical groups like the World Council of Churches and the Lausanne Movement, as well as denominations, have continued a dynamic and eclectic tradition of modern Protestant social teaching.

A clearer line of influence can be detected in the case of *Rerum Novarum* and Roman Catholic social teaching. A series of papal letters have been promulgated that are directly tied to Leo's 1891 encyclical, including letters on its fortieth (*Quadragesimo Anno*, 1931), seventieth (*Mater et Magistra*, 1961), eightieth (*Octogesima Adveniens*, 1971), and one hundredth (*Centesimus Annus*, 1991) anniversaries. Ideas that are nascent or implicit in *Rerum Novarum* are later developed and expressed in more detail, including some of the significant foundational principles surveyed in this introduction.

There is much to learn by engaging the particular principles we encounter in these texts, such as property, stewardship, subsidiarity, sphere sovereignty, solidarity, and sphere universality. The foundations of concepts like the preferential option for the poor and the shared emphasis on the importance of labor unions are also worth exploring. Leo and Kuyper both also recognize the international dimension of the social question even as they focus on the challenges endemic to individual nation-states. Beyond these particular themes, however, the more general method that Leo XIII and Kuyper employ is also instructive for Christian approaches to the social problems of today. In Kuyper's words, he engages in an "architectonic critique," by which he means an approach that questions and critically examines not just a particular problem or aspect of social life, but human life in its comprehensive totality. Thus, says Kuyper, "The social question is not a reality for you until you level an architectonic critique at human society as such and accordingly deem a different arrangement of the social order desirable, and also possible."[39]

The point of departure for such a comprehensive critique is the understanding of the human person. For both Leo XIII and Kuyper the relationship of humanity to God marks the major disjunction between Christian and other modern approaches. Kuyper identifies the rejection of the divine and the corresponding denial of humankind's created nature as key errors underlying all others. Thus, he says, "the individualistic character of the French Revolution is only a derived principle." In fact, that root principle is "humanity's emancipation from God and from the order instituted by him."[40] Both Leo and Kuyper identify an encroaching and increasingly virulent unbelief as characteristic of the modern social problem. Thus Leo warns: "Public institutions and the laws set aside the ancient religion."[41]

It may seem redundant or obvious, but it is critically important that Christian social thought begin with a specifically Christian conception of the human person in relationship to God, to others, and to the rest of creation. "Religion alone," says Leo, "can avail to destroy the evil at its root." Thus "all men should rest persuaded that the main thing needful is to re-establish Christian morals, apart from which all the plans and devices of the wisest will prove of little avail."[42] Only such a specifically religious perspective will allow the totality of human reality and its problems to be understood and provide the possibility of a coherent and comprehensive vision of social life.[43]

From this architectonic perspective we can then move to identifying general principles, such as solidarity and subsidiarity, and make prudential judgments about human society and the stewardship of creation and the development of culture. These prudential judgments depend on a great many things. It is not only important to properly identify and define the relevant principles. It is also necessary to diagnose and understand what the nature of the current situation is and what kind of action it calls for. Scientific study and engagement with the present-day are therefore required. This is a key place where Christian social thought dialogues with the physical and social sciences as well as the arts and trades. This is why Leo says, "Nothing is more useful than to look upon the world as it really is, and at the same time to seek elsewhere, as We have said, for the solace to its troubles."[44] This is likewise part of the founding vision for the Free University that Kuyper helped create, and the reason that he opens his social address by bemoaning the lack of scholarly inquiry into these pressing issues in Reformed circles, not only by theologians but also by specialists in political economy. Kuyper likewise concludes, "We too, for our part, ought to be engaged in study and action. We will not make any progress in tackling the social question with sentimental talk or shallow generalities."[45]

Many of the challenges that Leo and Kuyper faced in their day have a familiar feel to us today. Between then and now the Iron Curtain has risen and fallen, while collectivist regimes of various stripes continue to challenge the ideals and models of Western liberalism. Where economies were increasingly industrial and urban as opposed to agrarian and pastoral at the end of the nineteenth century, 125 years later we find economies developing in terms of communications technology and information. Questions of economic instability, inequality, and well-being have sharpened exponentially as globalization has seen increased international trade and cultural engagement as well as political conflict, civil unrest, and acts of terrorism. Concerns related to environmental stewardship have likewise increased as more people depend on economic growth and technological innovation to not only survive but also to move out of deprivation and poverty. The earth supports more people today than it ever has, and the moral stakes involved with economic growth and environmental stewardship have likewise never been greater.

The wisdom that Kuyper and Leo communicate in these texts is helpful for Christians today not only because they demonstrate intellectual rigor and a keen sense of the social question in their own time. They combine these virtues with fidelity to the Christian religion, and thus communicate timeless insights to us, and in so doing point beyond themselves to the first principles of Christian social thought. As Leo writes of social life, "to fall away from its primal constitution implies disease; to go back to it, recovery."[46] And, as Christ himself teaches us in the Gospel, our first and predominating concern must be God. When discussing concerns about material well-being, Christ exhorts his hearers: "Seek first the kingdom of God and his righteousness, and all these things will be added to you" (Matt 6:33 ESV). In the same way, Christians seeking to address the pressing social questions of today and tomorrow should follow the lead of Kuyper and Leo XIII, beginning with a proper understanding of God's will for human life and the constitutive nature of human identity created in the image of God.

Notes

1. Leo XIII, encyclical letter *Rerum Novarum* (May 15, 1891), §27.

2. The significance of the anniversary of these works has received some attention, including the publication of a Dutch volume including essays on and the texts of *Rerum Novarum* and Kuyper's "The Social Question and the Christian Religion." This volume was presented at the Christian Social Congress in Doorn, the Netherlands, held August 31–September 2, 2016. The journal *Faith & Economics* also published a theme issue focusing on Leo XIII, Abraham Kuyper, and Alfred Marshall, whose landmark *Principles of Economics* first appeared in 1890. See Rien Fraanje, ed., *Paus Leo XIII en Abraham Kuyper: De encycliek* Rerum Novarum *en de rede over de sociale kwestie* (Amsterdam: Boom, 2016); and *Faith & Economics* 67 (Spring 2016). Previous engagement with the legacies of Leo XIII and Abraham Kuyper include the proceedings of a conference held at Calvin College appearing in *Journal of Markets & Morality* 5, no. 1 (Spring 2002).

3. GDP per capita in 1800 in Germany was $986. By 1900 it was $2985. In the UK, this measure went from just over $2000 in 1800 to just under $4500 in 1900. France's GDP per capita was $1597 in 1850; fifty years later it was $2876. These figures are in 1990 international Geary-Khamis dollars, and appear in Max Roser, "GDP Growth Over the Last Centuries" (2016), published online at OurWorldInData.org, https://ourworldindata.org/gdp-growth-over-the-last-centuries/. The source for Roser's data is Clio Infra.

4. See Rondo Cameron, *Concise Economic History of the World: From Paleolithic Times to the Present*, 2nd ed. (New York: Oxford University Press, 1993), 193, Table 8-1.

5. See, for instance, "Christian Socialism," in *The Encyclopedia of Social Reform*, ed. William D. P. Bliss (New York: Funk & Wagnalls, 1897), 251–60.

6. Leo XIII, *Rerum Novarum*, §4.

7. Leo XIII, *Rerum Novarum*, §15.

8. The best biography of Kuyper is James Bratt, *Abraham Kuyper: Modern Calvinist, Christian Democrat* (Grand Rapids: Eerdmans, 2013). For Leo XIII, see Katherine Burton, *Leo XIII: The First Modern Pope* (New York: D. McKay, 1962). On the domestic political context of the Amsterdam congress, see Bratt, *Abraham Kuyper*, 221–23.

9. This was the first such congress held in the Netherlands, but was one of a broader social congress movement in Europe. See Clifford B. Anderson and Kenneth Woodrow Hale, "Meeting Together for the Good of the World: Christian Social Congresses Tried to Transform the Economic Order," *Christian History*, no. 104 (2013): 29–32. See also John Bolt, "Herman Bavinck's Contribution to Christian Social Consciousness," *Journal of Markets & Morality* 13, no. 2 (Fall 2010): 413–36, for a treatment of Christian social congresses as well as the contributions of Kuyper's younger colleague Herman Bavinck at the 1891 congress; and Herman Bavinck, "General Biblical Principles and the Relevance of Concrete Mosaic Law for the Social Question Today (1891)," *Journal of Markets & Morality* 10, no. 2 (Fall 2010): 437–46.

10. Although Leo's letter is more directly concerned with socialism, the connection between collectivist socialism and atomistic individualism is also recognized by Leo. See Dominique Rey, "The Meaning of *Rerum Novarum* for Western Europe Today," *Journal of Markets & Morality* 19, no. 2 (Fall 2016).

11. Kuyper, "The Social Question and the Christian Religion," 99n51.

12. Leo XIII, *Rerum Novarum*, §30.

13. Leo XIII, *Rerum Novarum*, §34.

14. It is appropriate to refer to a shared Christian understanding here because, as Kuyper himself notes, *Rerum Novarum* "dealt solely with those principles that all Christians hold in common and that we too share with our Roman Catholic fellow countrymen." See Kuyper, "The Social Question and the Christian Religion," 87n5.

15. Kuyper, "The Social Question and the Christian Religion," 60.

16. Leo XIII, *Rerum Novarum*, §34.

17. Leo XIII, *Rerum Novarum*, §19.

18. Leo XIII, *Rerum Novarum*, §15.

19. Leo XIII, *Rerum Novarum*, §7.

20. See Kuyper, "The Social Question and the Christian Religion," 67: "Absolute property rights have allowed immense fortunes to be amassed, which now form an insurmountable obstacle preventing society from doing justice to its sociological nature."

21. Leo XIII, *Rerum Novarum*, §22.

22. Kuyper, "The Social Question and the Christian Religion," 51.

23. Kuyper, "The Social Question and the Christian Religion," 74.

24. Kuyper, "The Social Question and the Christian Religion," 74.

25. Leo XIII, *Rerum Novarum*, §22.

26. Pius XI, encyclical letter *Quadragesimo Anno* (May 15, 1931), §79. The principle is also helpfully restated a century after *Rerum Novarum* in Pope John Paul II, encyclical letter *Centesimus Annus* (May 1, 1991), §49: "A community of a higher order should not interfere in the internal life of a community of a lower order, depriving the latter of its functions, but rather should support it in case of need and help to coordinate its activity with the activities of the rest of society, always with a view to the common good." See also Leo XIII, *Rerum Novarum*, §36: "The limits must be determined by the nature of the occasion which calls for the law's interference—the principle being that the law must not undertake more, nor proceed further, than is required for the remedy of the evil or the removal of the mischief."

27. Leo XIII, *Rerum Novarum*, §17.

28. Abraham Kuyper, "Sphere Sovereignty," in *Abraham Kuyper: A Centennial Reader*, ed. James D. Bratt (Grand Rapids: Eerdmans, 1998), 467–68.

29. See Kuyper, "The Social Question and the Christian Religion, 117n114: "It is perfectly true that if no help is forthcoming from elsewhere, the state must help. We are not allowed to let anyone die of hunger so long as bread still lies molding in so many breadboxes. Also, when the state helps it must do so quickly and adequately. (An indictment of our poor law!) But for that very reason it deserves emphasis that public relief is and remains, not our badge of honor, but a stinging indictment of the church and the rich—the consequence of a liberalism that undermined the strength of the church and made the rich egotistical." See also Leo XIII, *Rerum Novarum*, §55: "The State should watch over these societies of citizens banded together in accordance with their rights, but it should not thrust itself into their peculiar concerns and their organization, for things move and live by the spirit inspiring them, and may be killed by the rough grasp of a hand from without."

30. Leo XIII, *Rerum Novarum*, §25.

31. John Paul II, *Centesimus Annus*, §49: "In order to overcome today's widespread individualistic mentality, what is required is a *concrete commitment to solidarity and charity*, beginning in the family with the mutual support of husband and wife and the care which the different generations give to one another. In this sense the family too can be called a community of work and solidarity. It can happen, however, that when a family does decide to live up fully to its vocation, it finds itself without the necessary support from the State and without sufficient resources."

32. Kuyper, "The Social Question and the Christian Religion," 67. See also Abraham Kuyper, "Christ and the Needy (1895)," *Journal of Markets & Morality* 14, no. 2 (Fall 2011): 647–83.

33. Kuyper, "The Social Question and the Christian Religion," 82.

34. As Richard J. Mouw observes, "In the final analysis Kuyper was not as interested in looking for the connecting principles *within* the creation as he was in emphasizing the fact that the spheres are ultimately coordinated and linked by virtue of their mutual relationship to the transcendent will of the Creator." See Richard J. Mouw, *The Challenges of Cultural Discipleship: Essays in the Line of Abraham Kuyper* (Grand Rapids: Eerdmans, 2012), 53.

35. Leo XIII, *Rerum Novarum*, §21.

36. Paul VI, encyclical letter *Populorum Progressio* (March 26, 1967), §23.

37. Leo XIII, *Rerum Novarum*, §44. See also Pontifical Council for Justice and Peace, *Compendium of the Social Doctrine of the Church* (Vatican City: Libreria Editrice Vaticana, 2004), part one, chapter IV, section 3, on the universal destination of goods; and Manfred Spieker, "The Universal Destination of Goods: The Ethics of Property in the Theory of a Christian Society," *Journal of Markets & Morality* 8, no. 2 (Fall 2005): 333–54.

38. See Rolf van der Woude, "Taming the Beast: The Long and Hard Road to the Christian Social Conference of 1952," *Journal of Markets & Morality* 14, no. 2 (Fall 2011): 419–44.

39. Kuyper, "The Social Question and the Christian Religion," 65.

40. Kuyper, "The Social Question and the Christian Religion," 70.

41. Leo XIII, *Rerum Novarum*, §3.

42. Leo XIII, *Rerum Novarum*, §62.

43. See also Kuyper, "The Social Question and the Christian Religion," 73: "Today, everything has to be a free product of human creativity. The social edifice has to be erected according to man's whim and caprice. That is why God has to go, so that men, no longer restrained by natural bonds, can invert every moral precept into its opposite and subvert every pillar of human society. Does that not point us in the direction we ought to go precisely when dealing with the social question? As Christians we are to emphasize as strongly as possible the majesty of God's authority and the absolute validity of his ordinances. For all our condemnation of the rotting structure of our society, we are never to help erect any structure other than one that rests on the foundation laid by God."

44. Leo XIII, *Rerum Novarum*, §18.

45. Kuyper, "The Social Question and the Christian Religion," 110n95.

46. Leo XIII, *Rerum Novarum*, §27.

RERUM NOVARUM

Text Introduction

This encyclical letter was promulgated by Pope Leo XIII on May 15, 1891. The encyclical opens by describing its subject matter as the relationship between "capital and labor." In his introduction to the encyclical, Étienne Gilson expanded on this by using the title, "Rights and Duties of Capital and Labor." He observes in his introduction that the encyclical letter "has been given various titles," and notes as well that the titles "On the Condition of the Working Classes" and "The Worker's Charter" are also warranted given the major occasion for the letter. The occasion for the letter, which forms the foundation for more than a century of subsequent Roman Catholic social teaching, is the social upheaval following industrialization, urbanization, and liberalization. Leo takes on socialism, a dominant proposed solution, by asserting the priority of private property and ownership, the mutual obligations and dependence of workers and owners, and the religious foundations for a proper conception of the relationship between labor and capital as well as of the social order more broadly. Gilson added some references and observations in his edition, which are retained and denoted in this edition by brackets. Alternative readings and variants are also included in Gilson's edition, which should be consulted for those scholarly purposes.

Source: Leo XIII. Encyclical Letter *Rerum Novarum* (May 15, 1891). In *The Church Speaks to the Modern World: The Social Teachings of Leo XIII*, edited, annotated and with an introduction by Étienne Gilson, 205–44. Garden City, NY: Image, 1954. Reprinted with permission © Libreria Editrice Vaticana.

Rerum Novarum

Encyclical of Pope Leo XIII
On Capital and Labor

To Our Venerable Brethren the Patriarchs,
Primates, Archbishops, Bishops, and other ordinaries
of places having Peace and Communion with the Apostolic See.

Rights and Duties of Capital and Labor

1. That the spirit of revolutionary change, which has long been disturbing the nations of the world, should have passed beyond the sphere of politics and made its influence felt in the cognate sphere of practical economics is not surprising. The elements of the conflict now raging are unmistakable, in the vast expansion of industrial pursuits and the marvellous discoveries of science; in the changed relations between masters and workmen; in the enormous fortunes of some few individuals, and the utter poverty of the masses; in the increased self-reliance and closer mutual combination of the working classes; as also, finally, in the prevailing moral degeneracy. The momentous gravity of the state of things now obtaining fills every mind with painful apprehension; wise men are discussing it; practical men are proposing schemes; popular meetings, legislatures, and rulers of nations are all busied with it—actually there is no question which has taken deeper hold on the public mind.

2. Therefore, venerable brethren, as on former occasions when it seemed opportune to refute false teaching, We have addressed you in the interests of the Church and of the common weal, and have issued letters bearing on political power, human liberty, the Christian constitution of the State, and like matters, so have We thought it expedient now to speak on the condition of the working classes.[1] It is a subject on which We have already touched more than once, incidentally. But in the present letter, the responsibility of the apostolic office urges Us to treat the question of set purpose and in detail, in order that no misapprehension may exist as to the principles which truth and justice dictate for its settlement. The discussion is not easy, nor is it void of danger. It is no easy matter to define the relative rights and mutual duties of the rich and of the poor, of capital and of labor. And the danger lies in this, that crafty agitators are intent on making use of these differences of opinion to pervert men's judgments and to stir up the people to revolt.

3. In any case we clearly see, and on this there is general agreement, that some opportune remedy must be found quickly for the misery and wretchedness pressing so unjustly on the majority of the working class: for the ancient workingmen's guilds were abolished in the last century, and no other protective organization took their place. Public institutions and the laws set aside the ancient religion. Hence, by degrees it has come to pass that working men have been surrendered, isolated and helpless, to the hard-heartedness of employers and the greed of unchecked competition. The mischief has been increased by rapacious usury, which, although more than once condemned by the Church, is nevertheless, under a different guise, but with like injustice, still practiced by covetous and grasping men. To this must be added that the hiring of labor and the conduct of trade are concentrated in the hands of comparatively few; so that a small number of very rich men have been able to lay upon the teeming masses of the laboring poor a yoke little better than that of slavery itself.

4. To remedy these wrongs the socialists, working on the poor man's envy of the rich, are striving to do away with private property, and contend that individual possessions should become the common property of all, to be administered by the

State or by municipal bodies. They hold that by thus transferring property from private individuals to the community, the present mischievous state of things will be set to rights, inasmuch as each citizen will then get his fair share of whatever there is to enjoy. But their contentions are so clearly powerless to end the controversy that were they carried into effect the working man himself would be among the first to suffer. They are, moreover, emphatically unjust, for they would rob the lawful possessor, distort the functions of the State, and create utter confusion in the community.

5. It is surely undeniable that, when a man engages in remunerative labor, the impelling reason and motive of his work is to obtain property, and thereafter to hold it as his very own. If one man hires out to another his strength or skill, he does so for the purpose of receiving in return what is necessary for the satisfaction of his needs; he therefore expressly intends to acquire a right full and real, not only to the remuneration, but also to the disposal of such remuneration, just as he pleases. Thus, if he lives sparingly, saves money, and, for greater security, invests his savings in land, the land, in such case, is only his wages under another form; and, consequently, a working man's little estate thus purchased should be as completely at his full disposal as are the wages he receives for his labor. But it is precisely in such power of disposal that ownership obtains, whether the property consist of land or chattels. Socialists, therefore, by endeavoring to transfer the possessions of individuals to the community at large, strike at the interests of every wage-earner, since they would deprive him of the liberty of disposing of his wages, and thereby of all hope and possibility of increasing his resources and of bettering his condition in life.

6. What is of far greater moment, however, is the fact that the remedy they propose is manifestly against justice. For, every man has by nature the right to possess property as his own. This is one of the chief points of distinction between man and the animal creation, for the brute has no power of self-direction, but is governed by two main instincts, which keep his powers on the alert, impel him to develop them in a fitting manner, and stimulate and determine him to action without any power

of choice. One of these instincts is self-preservation, the other the propagation of the species. Both can attain their purpose by means of things which lie within range; beyond their verge the brute creation cannot go, for they are moved to action by their senses only, and in the special direction which these suggest. But with man it is wholly different. He possesses, on the one hand, the full perfection of the animal being, and hence enjoys at least as much as the rest of the animal kind, the fruition of things material. But animal nature, however perfect, is far from representing the human being in its completeness, and is in truth but humanity's humble handmaid, made to serve and to obey. It is the mind, or reason, which is the predominant element in us who are human creatures; it is this which renders a human being human, and distinguishes him essentially from the brute. And on this very account—that man alone among the animal creation is endowed with reason—it must be within his right to possess things not merely for temporary and momentary use, as other living things do, but to have and to hold them in stable and permanent possession; he must have not only things that perish in the use, but those also which, though they have been reduced into use, continue for further use in after time.

7. This becomes still more clearly evident if man's nature be considered a little more deeply. For man, fathoming by his faculty of reason matters without number, linking the future with the present, and being master of his own acts, guides his ways under the eternal law and the power of God, whose providence governs all things. Wherefore, it is in his power to exercise his choice not only as to matters that regard his present welfare, but also about those which he deems may be for his advantage in time yet to come. Hence, man not only should possess the fruits of the earth, but also the very soil, inasmuch as from the produce of the earth he has to lay by provision for the future. Man's needs do not die out, but forever recur; although satisfied today, they demand fresh supplies for tomorrow. Nature accordingly must have given to man a source that is stable and remaining always with him, from which he might look to draw continual supplies. And this stable condition of things he finds solely in the earth and its fruits. There is no need to bring in the State.

Man precedes the State, and possesses, prior to the formation of any State, the right of providing for the substance of his body.

8. The fact that God has given the earth for the use and enjoyment of the whole human race can in no way be a bar to the owning of private property. For God has granted the earth to mankind in general, not in the sense that all without distinction can deal with it as they like, but rather that no part of it was assigned to any one in particular, and that the limits of private possession have been left to be fixed by man's own industry, and by the laws of individual races. Moreover, the earth, even though apportioned among private owners, ceases not thereby to minister to the needs of all, inasmuch as there is not one who does not sustain life from what the land produces. Those who do not possess the soil contribute their labor; hence, it may truly be said that all human subsistence is derived either from labor on one's own land, or from some toil, some calling, which is paid for either in the produce of the land itself, or in that which is exchanged for what the land brings forth.

9. Here, again, we have further proof that private ownership is in accordance with the law of nature. Truly, that which is required for the preservation of life, and for life's well-being, is produced in great abundance from the soil, but not until man has brought it into cultivation and expended upon it his solicitude and skill. Now, when man thus turns the activity of his mind and the strength of his body toward procuring the fruits of nature, by such act he makes his own that portion of nature's field which he cultivates—that portion on which he leaves, as it were, the impress of his personality; and it cannot but be just that he should possess that portion as his very own, and have a right to hold it without any one being justified in violating that right.

10. So strong and convincing are these arguments that it seems amazing that some should now be setting up anew certain obsolete opinions in opposition to what is here laid down. They assert that it is right for private persons to have the use of the soil and its various fruits, but that it is unjust for any one to possess outright either the land on which he has built or the estate which he has brought under cultivation. But those who deny these rights do not perceive that they are defrauding man

of what his own labor has produced. For the soil which is tilled and cultivated with toil and skill utterly changes its condition; it was wild before, now it is fruitful; was barren, but now brings forth in abundance. That which has thus altered and improved the land becomes so truly part of itself as to be in great measure indistinguishable and inseparable from it. Is it just that the fruit of a man's own sweat and labor should be possessed and enjoyed by any one else? As effects follow their cause, so is it just and right that the results of labor should belong to those who have bestowed their labor.

11. With reason, then, the common opinion of mankind, little affected by the few dissentients who have contended for the opposite view, has found in the careful study of nature, and in the laws of nature, the foundations of the division of property, and the practice of all ages has consecrated the principle of private ownership, as being pre-eminently in conformity with human nature, and as conducing in the most unmistakable manner to the peace and tranquillity of human existence. The same principle is confirmed and enforced by the civil laws—laws which, so long as they are just, derive from the law of nature their binding force. The authority of the divine law adds its sanction, forbidding us in severest terms even to covet that which is another's: "Thou shalt not covet thy neighbour's wife; nor his house, nor his field, nor his man-servant, nor his maid-servant, nor his ox, nor his ass, nor anything that is his."[2]

12. The rights here spoken of, belonging to each individual man, are seen in much stronger light when considered in relation to man's social and domestic obligations. In choosing a state of life, it is indisputable that all are at full liberty to follow the counsel of Jesus Christ as to observing virginity, or to bind themselves by the marriage tie. No human law can abolish the natural and original right of marriage, nor in any way limit the chief and principal purpose of marriage ordained by God's authority from the beginning: "Increase and multiply."[3] Hence we have the family, the "society" of a man's house—a society very small, one must admit, but none the less a true society, and one older than any State. Consequently, it has rights and duties peculiar to itself which are quite independent of the State.

13. That right to property, therefore, which has been proved to belong naturally to individual persons, must in like wise belong to a man in his capacity of head of a family; nay, that right is all the stronger in proportion as the human person receives a wider extension in the family group. It is a most sacred law of nature that a father should provide food and all necessaries for those whom he has begotten; and, similarly, it is natural that he should wish that his children, who carry on, so to speak, and continue his personality, should be by him provided with all that is needful to enable them to keep themselves decently from want and misery amid the uncertainties of this mortal life. Now, in no other way can a father effect this except by the ownership of productive property, which he can transmit to his children by inheritance. A family, no less than a State, is, as We have said, a true society, governed by an authority peculiar to itself, that is to say, by the authority of the father. Provided, therefore, the limits which are prescribed by the very purposes for which it exists be not transgressed, the family has at least equal rights with the State in the choice and pursuit of the things needful to its preservation and its just liberty. We say, "at least equal rights"; for, inasmuch as the domestic household is antecedent, as well in idea as in fact, to the gathering of men into a community, the family must necessarily have rights and duties which are prior to those of the community, and founded more immediately in nature. If the citizens, if the families on entering into association and fellowship, were to experience hindrance in a commonwealth instead of help, and were to find their rights attacked instead of being upheld, society would rightly be an object of detestation rather than of desire.

14. The contention, then, that the civil government should at its option intrude into and exercise intimate control over the family and the household is a great and pernicious error. True, if a family finds itself in exceeding distress, utterly deprived of the counsel of friends, and without any prospect of extricating itself, it is right that extreme necessity be met by public aid, since each family is a part of the commonwealth. In like manner, if within the precincts of the household there occur grave disturbance of mutual rights, public authority should intervene to force each

party to yield to the other its proper due; for this is not to deprive citizens of their rights, but justly and properly to safeguard and strengthen them. But the rulers of the commonwealth must go no further; here, nature bids them stop. Paternal authority can be neither abolished nor absorbed by the State; for it has the same source as human life itself. "The child belongs to the father," and is, as it were, the continuation of the father's personality; and speaking strictly, the child takes its place in civil society, not of its own right, but in its quality as member of the family in which it is born. And for the very reason that "the child belongs to the father" it is, as St. Thomas Aquinas says, "before it attains the use of free will, under the power and the charge of its parents."[4] The socialists, therefore, in setting aside the parent and setting up a State supervision, act against natural justice, and destroy the structure of the home.

15. And in addition to injustice, it is only too evident what an upset and disturbance there would be in all classes, and to how intolerable and hateful a slavery citizens would be subjected. The door would be thrown open to envy, to mutual invective, and to discord; the sources of wealth themselves would run dry, for no one would have any interest in exerting his talents or his industry; and that ideal equality about which they entertain pleasant dreams would be in reality the levelling down of all to a like condition of misery and degradation.

Hence, it is clear that the main tenet of socialism, community of goods, must be utterly rejected, since it only injures those whom it would seem meant to benefit, is directly contrary to the natural rights of mankind, and would introduce confusion and disorder into the commonweal. The first and most fundamental principle, therefore, if one would undertake to alleviate the condition of the masses, must be the inviolability of private property. This being established, we proceed to show where the remedy sought for must be found.

16. We approach the subject with confidence, and in the exercise of the rights which manifestly appertain to Us, for no practical solution of this question will be found apart from the intervention of religion and of the Church. It is We who are the chief guardian of religion and the chief dispenser of what per-

tains to the Church; and by keeping silence we would seem to neglect the duty incumbent on us. Doubtless, this most serious question demands the attention and the efforts of others besides ourselves—to wit, of the rulers of States, of employers of labor, of the wealthy, aye, of the working classes themselves, for whom We are pleading. But We affirm without hesitation that all the striving of men will be vain if they leave out the Church. It is the Church that insists, on the authority of the Gospel, upon those teachings whereby the conflict can be brought to an end, or rendered, at least, far less bitter; the Church uses her efforts not only to enlighten the mind, but to direct by her precepts the life and conduct of each and all; the Church improves and betters the condition of the working man by means of numerous organizations; does her best to enlist the services of all classes in discussing and endeavoring to further in the most practical way, the interests of the working classes; and considers that for this purpose recourse should be had, in due measure and degree, to the intervention of the law and of State authority.

17. It must be first of all recognized that the condition of things inherent in human affairs must be borne with, for it is impossible to reduce civil society to one dead level. Socialists may in that intent do their utmost, but all striving against nature is in vain. There naturally exist among mankind manifold differences of the most important kind; people differ in capacity, skill, health, strength; and unequal fortune is a necessary result of unequal condition. Such unequality is far from being disadvantageous either to individuals or to the community. Social and public life can only be maintained by means of various kinds of capacity for business and the playing of many parts; and each man, as a rule, chooses the part which suits his own peculiar domestic condition. As regards bodily labor, even had man never fallen from the state of innocence, he would not have remained wholly idle; but that which would then have been his free choice and his delight became afterwards compulsory, and the painful expiation for his disobedience. "Cursed be the earth in thy work; in thy labor thou shalt eat of it all the days of thy life."[5]

18. In like manner, the other pains and hardships of life will have no end or cessation on earth; for the consequences of sin

are bitter and hard to bear, and they must accompany man so long as life lasts. To suffer and to endure, therefore, is the lot of humanity; let them strive as they may, no strength and no artifice will ever succeed in banishing from human life the ills and troubles which beset it. If any there are who pretend differently—who hold out to a hard-pressed people the boon of freedom from pain and trouble, an undisturbed repose, and constant enjoyment—they delude the people and impose upon them, and their lying promises will only one day bring forth evils worse than the present. Nothing is more useful than to look upon the world as it really is, and at the same time to seek elsewhere, as We have said, for the solace to its troubles.

19. The great mistake made in regard to the matter now under consideration is to take up with the notion that class is naturally hostile to class, and that the wealthy and the working men are intended by nature to live in mutual conflict. So irrational and so false is this view that the direct contrary is the truth. Just as the symmetry of the human frame is the result of the suitable arrangement of the different parts of the body, so in a State is it ordained by nature that these two classes should dwell in harmony and agreement, so as to maintain the balance of the body politic. Each needs the other: capital cannot do without labor, nor labor without capital. Mutual agreement results in the beauty of good order, while perpetual conflict necessarily produces confusion and savage barbarity. Now, in preventing such strife as this, and in uprooting it, the efficacy of Christian institutions is marvellous and manifold. First of all, there is no intermediary more powerful than religion (whereof the Church is the interpreter and guardian) in drawing the rich and the working class together, by reminding each of its duties to the other, and especially of the obligations of justice.

20. Of these duties, the following bind the proletarian and the worker: fully and faithfully to perform the work which has been freely and equitably agreed upon; never to injure the property, nor to outrage the person, of an employer; never to resort to violence in defending their own cause, nor to engage in riot or disorder; and to have nothing to do with men of evil principles, who work upon the people with artful promises of great results,

and excite foolish hopes which usually end in useless regrets and grievous loss. The following duties bind the wealthy owner and the employer: not to look upon their work people as their bondsmen, but to respect in every man his dignity as a person ennobled by Christian character. They are reminded that, according to natural reason and Christian philosophy, working for gain is creditable, not shameful, to a man, since it enables him to earn an honorable livelihood; but to misuse men as though they were things in the pursuit of gain, or to value them solely for their physical powers—that is truly shameful and inhuman. Again justice demands that, in dealing with the working man, religion and the good of his soul must be kept in mind. Hence, the employer is bound to see that the worker has time for his religious duties; that he be not exposed to corrupting influences and dangerous occasions; and that he be not led away to neglect his home and family, or to squander his earnings. Furthermore, the employer must never tax his work people beyond their strength, or employ them in work unsuited to their sex and age. His great and principal duty is to give every one what is just. Doubtless, before deciding whether wages are fair, many things have to be considered; but wealthy owners and all masters of labor should be mindful of this—that to exercise pressure upon the indigent and the destitute for the sake of gain, and to gather one's profit out of the need of another, is condemned by all laws, human and divine. To defraud any one of wages that are his due is a great crime which cries to the avenging anger of Heaven. "Behold, the hire of the laborers ... which by fraud has been kept back by you, crieth; and the cry of them hath entered into the ears of the Lord of Sabaoth."[6] Lastly, the rich must religiously refrain from cutting down the workmen's earnings, whether by force, by fraud, or by usurious dealing; and with all the greater reason because the laboring man is, as a rule, weak and unprotected, and because his slender means should in proportion to their scantiness be accounted sacred.

Were these precepts carefully obeyed and followed out, would they not be sufficient of themselves to keep under all strife and all its causes?

21. But the Church, with Jesus Christ as her Master and Guide, aims higher still. She lays down precepts yet more perfect, and tries to bind class to class in friendliness and good feeling. The things of earth cannot be understood or valued aright without taking into consideration the life to come, the life that will know no death. Exclude the idea of futurity, and forthwith the very notion of what is good and right would perish; nay, the whole scheme of the universe would become a dark and unfathomable mystery. The great truth which we learn from nature herself is also the grand Christian dogma on which religion rests as on its foundation—that, when we have given up this present life, then shall we really begin to live. God has not created us for the perishable and transitory things of earth, but for things heavenly and everlasting; He has given us this world as a place of exile, and not as our abiding place. As for riches and the other things which men call good and desirable, whether we have them in abundance, or are lacking in them—so far as eternal happiness is concerned—it makes no difference; the only important thing is to use them aright. Jesus Christ, when He redeemed us with plentiful redemption, took not away the pains and sorrows which in such large proportion are woven together in the web of our mortal life. He transformed them into motives of virtue and occasions of merit; and no man can hope for eternal reward unless he follow in the blood-stained footprints of his Saviour. "If we suffer with Him, we shall also reign with Him."[7] Christ's labors and sufferings, accepted of His own free will, have marvellously sweetened all suffering and all labor. And not only by His example, but by His grace and by the hope held forth of everlasting recompense, has He made pain and grief more easy to endure; "for that which is at present momentary and light of our tribulation, worketh for us above measure exceedingly an eternal weight of glory."[8]

22. Therefore, those whom fortune favors are warned that riches do not bring freedom from sorrow and are of no avail for eternal happiness, but rather are obstacles;[9] that the rich should tremble at the threatenings of Jesus Christ—threatenings so unwonted in the mouth of our Lord[10]—and that a most strict account must be given to the Supreme Judge for all we

possess. The chief and most excellent rule for the right use of money is one the heathen philosophers hinted at, but which the Church has traced out clearly, and has not only made known to men's minds, but has impressed upon their lives. It rests on the principle that it is one thing to have a right to the possession of money and another to have a right to use money as one wills. Private ownership, as we have seen, is the natural right of man, and to exercise that right, especially as members of society, is not only lawful, but absolutely necessary. "It is lawful," says St. Thomas Aquinas, "for a man to hold private property; and it is also necessary for the carrying on of human existence."[11] But if the question be asked: How must one's possessions be used?—the Church replies without hesitation in the words of the same holy Doctor: "Man should not consider his material possessions as his own, but as common to all, so as to share them without hesitation when others are in need. Whence the Apostle with, 'Command the rich of this world ... to offer with no stint, to apportion largely.'"[12] True, no one is commanded to distribute to others that which is required for his own needs and those of his household; nor even to give away what is reasonably required to keep up becomingly his condition in life, "for no one ought to live other than becomingly."[13] But, when what necessity demands has been supplied, and one's standing fairly taken thought for, it becomes a duty to give to the indigent out of what remains over. "Of that which remaineth, give alms."[14] It is a duty, not of justice (save in extreme cases), but of Christian charity—a duty not enforced by human law. But the laws and judgments of men must yield place to the laws and judgments of Christ the true God, who in many ways urges on His followers the practice of almsgiving—"It is more blessed to give than to receive";[15] and who will count a kindness done or refused to the poor as done or refused to Himself—"As long as you did it to one of My least brethren you did it to Me."[16] To sum up, then, what has been said: Whoever has received from the divine bounty a large share of temporal blessings, whether they be external and material, or gifts of the mind, has received them for the purpose of using them for the perfecting of his own nature, and, at the same time, that he may employ them, as the steward of God's providence, for the benefit of others. "He that hath a talent," said St. Gregory the Great, "let him see that he hide it not; he that hath abundance, let him quicken himself to mercy and generosity; he that hath art and skill, let him do his best to share the use and the utility hereof with his neighbor."[17]

23. As for those who possess not the gifts of fortune, they are taught by the Church that in God's sight poverty is no disgrace, and that there is nothing to be ashamed of in earning their bread by labor. This is enforced by what we see in Christ Himself, who, "whereas He was rich, for our sakes became poor";[18] and who, being the Son of God, and God Himself, chose to seem and to be considered the son of a carpenter—nay, did not disdain to spend a great part of His life as a carpenter Himself. "Is not this the carpenter, the son of Mary?"[19]

24. From contemplation of this divine Model, it is more easy to understand that the true worth and nobility of man lie in his moral qualities, that is, in virtue; that virtue is, moreover, the common inheritance of men, equally within the reach of high and low, rich and poor; and that virtue, and virtue alone, wherever found, will be followed by the rewards of everlasting happiness. Nay, God Himself seems to incline rather to those who suffer misfortune; for Jesus Christ calls the poor "blessed";[20] He lovingly invites those in labor and grief to come to Him for solace;[21] and He displays the tenderest charity toward the lowly and the oppressed. These reflections cannot fail to keep down the pride of the well-to-do, and to give heart to the unfortunate; to move the former to be generous and the latter to be moderate in their desires. Thus, the separation which pride would set up tends to disappear, nor will it be difficult to make rich and poor join hands in friendly concord.

25. But, if Christian precepts prevail, the respective classes will not only be united in the bonds of friendship, but also in those of brotherly love. For they will understand and feel that all men are children of the same common Father, who is God; that all have alike the same last end, which is God Himself, who alone can make either men or angels absolutely and perfectly happy; that each and all are redeemed and made sons of God, by Jesus Christ, "the first-born among many brethren"; that the blessings of nature and the gifts of grace belong to the whole human race

in common, and that from none except the unworthy is withheld the inheritance of the kingdom of Heaven. "If sons, heirs also; heirs indeed of God, and co-heirs with Christ."[22]

Such is the scheme of duties and of rights which is shown forth to the world by the Gospel. Would it not seem that, were society penetrated with ideas like these, strife must quickly cease?

26. But the Church, not content with pointing out the remedy, also applies it. For the Church does her utmost to teach and to train men, and to educate them and by the intermediary of her bishops and clergy diffuses her salutary teachings far and wide. She strives to influence the mind and the heart so that all may willingly yield themselves to be formed and guided by the commandments of God. It is precisely in this fundamental and momentous matter, on which everything depends that the Church possesses a power peculiarly her own. The instruments which she employs are given to her by Jesus Christ Himself for the very purpose of reaching the hearts of men, and derive their efficiency from God. They alone can reach the innermost heart and conscience, and bring men to act from a motive of duty, to control their passions and appetites, to love God and their fellow men with a love that is outstanding and of the highest degree and to break down courageously every barrier which blocks the way to virtue.

27. On this subject we need but recall for one moment the examples recorded in history. Of these facts there cannot be any shadow of doubt: for instance, that civil society was renovated in every part by Christian institutions; that in the strength of that renewal the human race was lifted up to better things—nay, that it was brought back from death to life, and to so excellent a life that nothing more perfect had been known before, or will come to be known in the ages that have yet to be. Of this beneficent transformation Jesus Christ was at once the first cause and the final end; as from Him all came, so to Him was all to be brought back. For, when the human race, by the light of the Gospel message, came to know the grand mystery of the Incarnation of the Word and the redemption of man, at once the life of Jesus Christ, God and Man, pervaded every race and nation, and interpenetrated them with His faith, His precepts, and His laws. And

if human society is to be healed now, in no other way can it be healed save by a return to Christian life and Christian institutions. When a society is perishing, the wholesome advice to give to those who would restore it is to call it to the principles from which it sprang; for the purpose and perfection of an association is to aim at and to attain that for which it is formed, and its efforts should be put in motion and inspired by the end and object which originally gave it being. Hence, to fall away from its primal constitution implies disease; to go back to it, recovery. And this may be asserted with utmost truth both of the whole body of the commonwealth and of that class of its citizens—by far the great majority—who get their living by their labor.

28. Neither must it be supposed that the solicitude of the Church is so preoccupied with the spiritual concerns of her children as to neglect their temporal and earthly interests. Her desire is that the poor, for example, should rise above poverty and wretchedness, and better their condition in life; and for this she makes a strong endeavor. By the fact that she calls men to virtue and forms them to its practice she promotes this in no slight degree. Christian morality, when adequately and completely practiced, leads of itself to temporal prosperity, for it merits the blessing of that God who is the source of all blessings; it powerfully restrains the greed of possession and the thirst for pleasure—twin plagues, which too often make a man who is void of self-restraint miserable in the midst of abundance;[23] it makes men supply for the lack of means through economy, teaching them to be content with frugal living, and further, keeping them out of the reach of those vices which devour not small incomes merely, but large fortunes, and dissipate many a goodly inheritance.

29. The Church, moreover, intervenes directly in behalf of the poor, by setting on foot and maintaining many associations which she knows to be efficient for the relief of poverty. Herein, again, she has always succeeded so well as to have even extorted the praise of her enemies. Such was the ardor of brotherly love among the earliest Christians that numbers of those who were in better circumstances despoiled themselves of their possessions in order to relieve their brethren; whence "neither was there any one needy among them."[24] To the order of deacons, instituted

in that very intent, was committed by the Apostles the charge of the daily doles; and the Apostle Paul, though burdened with the solicitude of all the churches, hesitated not to undertake laborious journeys in order to carry the alms of the faithful to the poorer Christians. Tertullian calls these contributions, given voluntarily by Christians in their assemblies, deposits of piety, because, to cite his own words, they were employed "in feeding the needy, in burying them, in support of youths and maidens destitute of means and deprived of their parents, in the care of the aged, and the relief of the shipwrecked."[25]

30. Thus, by degrees, came into existence the patrimony which the Church has guarded with religious care as the inheritance of the poor. Nay, in order to spare them the shame of begging, the Church has provided aid for the needy. The common Mother of rich and poor has aroused everywhere the heroism of charity, and has established congregations of religious and many other useful institutions for help and mercy, so that hardly any kind of suffering could exist which was not afforded relief. At the present day many there are who, like the heathen of old, seek to blame and condemn the Church for such eminent charity. They would substitute in its stead a system of relief organized by the State. But no human expedients will ever make up for the devotedness and self-sacrifice of Christian charity. Charity, as a virtue, pertains to the Church; for virtue it is not, unless it be drawn from the Most Sacred Heart of Jesus Christ; and whosoever turns his back on the Church cannot be near to Christ.

31. It cannot, however, be doubted that to attain the purpose we are treating of, not only the Church, but all human agencies, must concur. All who are concerned in the matter should be of one mind and according to their ability act together. It is with this, as with providence that governs the world; the results of causes do not usually take place save where all the causes co-operate.

It is sufficient, therefore, to inquire what part the State should play in the work of remedy and relief.

32. By the State we here understand, not the particular form of government prevailing in this or that nation, but the State as rightly apprehended; that is to say, any government conformable in its institutions to right reason and natural law, and to those

dictates of the divine wisdom which we have expounded in the encyclical *On the Christian Constitution of the State*.[26] The foremost duty, therefore, of the rulers of the State should be to make sure that the laws and institutions, the general character and administration of the commonwealth, shall be such as of themselves to realize public well-being and private prosperity. This is the proper scope of wise statesmanship and is the work of the rulers. Now a State chiefly prospers and thrives through moral rule, well-regulated family life, respect for religion and justice, the moderation and fair imposing of public taxes, the progress of the arts and of trade, the abundant yield of the land—through everything, in fact, which makes the citizens better and happier. Hereby, then, it lies in the power of a ruler to benefit every class in the State, and amongst the rest to promote to the utmost the interests of the poor; and this in virtue of his office, and without being open to suspicion of undue interference—since it is the province of the commonwealth to serve the common good. And the more that is done for the benefit of the working classes by the general laws of the country, the less need will there be to seek for special means to relieve them.

33. There is another and deeper consideration which must not be lost sight of. As regards the State, the interests of all, whether high or low, are equal. The members of the working classes are citizens by nature and by the same right as the rich; they are real parts, living the life which makes up, through the family, the body of the commonwealth; and it need hardly be said that they are in every city very largely in the majority. It would be irrational to neglect one portion of the citizens and favor another, and therefore the public administration must duly and solicitously provide for the welfare and the comfort of the working classes; otherwise, that law of justice will be violated which ordains that each man shall have his due. To cite the wise words of St. Thomas Aquinas: "As the part and the whole are in a certain sense identical, so that which belongs to the whole in a sense belongs to the part."[27] Among the many and grave duties of rulers who would do their best for the people, the first

and chief is to act with strict justice—with that justice which is called *distributive*—toward each and every class alike.

34. But although all citizens, without exception, can and ought to contribute to that common good in which individuals share so advantageously to themselves, yet it should not be supposed that all can contribute in the like way and to the same extent. No matter what changes may occur in forms of government, there will ever be differences and inequalities of condition in the State. Society cannot exist or be conceived of without them. Some there must be who devote themselves to the work of the commonwealth, who make the laws or administer justice, or whose advice and authority govern the nation in times of peace, and defend it in war. Such men clearly occupy the foremost place in the State, and should be held in highest estimation, for their work concerns most nearly and effectively the general interests of the community. Those who labor at a trade or calling do not promote the general welfare in such measure as this, but they benefit the nation, if less directly, in a most important manner. We have insisted, it is true, that, since the end of society is to make men better, the chief good that society can possess is virtue. Nevertheless, it is the business of a well-constituted body politic to see to the provision of those material and external helps "the use of which is necessary to virtuous action."²⁸ Now, for the provision of such commodities, the labor of the working class—the exercise of their skill, and the employment of their strength, in the cultivation of the land, and in the workshops of trade—is especially responsible and quite indispensable. Indeed, their co-operation is in this respect so important that it may be truly said that it is only by the labor of working men that States grow rich. Justice, therefore, demands that the interests of the working classes should be carefully watched over by the administration, so that they who contribute so largely to the advantage of the community may themselves share in the benefits which they create—that being housed, clothed, and bodily fit, they may find their life less hard and more endurable. It follows that whatever shall appear to prove conducive to the well-being of those who work should obtain favorable consideration. There is no fear

that solicitude of this kind will be harmful to any interest; on the contrary, it will be to the advantage of all, for it cannot but be good for the commonwealth to shield from misery those on whom it so largely depends for the things that it needs.

35. We have said that the State must not absorb the individual or the family; both should be allowed free and untrammelled action so far as is consistent with the common good and the interest of others. Rulers should, nevertheless, anxiously safeguard the community and all its members; the community, because the conservation thereof is so emphatically the business of the supreme power, that the safety of the commonwealth is not only the first law, but it is a government's whole reason of existence; and the members, because both philosophy and the Gospel concur in laying down that the object of the government of the State should be, not the advantage of the ruler, but the benefit of those over whom he is placed. As the power to rule comes from God, and is, as it were, a participation in His, the highest of all sovereignties, it should be exercised as the power of God is exercised—with a fatherly solicitude which not only guides the whole, but reaches also individuals.

36. Whenever the general interest or any particular class suffers, or is threatened with harm, which can in no other way be met or prevented, the public authority must step in to deal with it. Now, it is to the interest of the community, as well as of the individual, that peace and good order should be maintained; that all things should be carried on in accordance with God's laws and those of nature; that the discipline of family life should be observed and that religion should be obeyed; that a high standard of morality should prevail, both in public and private life; that justice should be held sacred and that no one should injure another with impunity; that the members of the commonwealth should grow up to man's estate strong and robust, and capable, if need be, of guarding and defending their country. If by a strike of workers or concerted interruption of work there should be imminent danger of disturbance to the public peace; or if circumstances were such as that among the working class the ties of family life were relaxed; if religion were found to suffer through the workers not having time and opportunity afforded

them to practice its duties; if in workshops and factories there were danger to morals through the mixing of the sexes or from other harmful occasions of evil; or if employers laid burdens upon their workmen which were unjust, or degraded them with conditions repugnant to their dignity as human beings; finally, if health were endangered by excessive labor, or by work unsuited to sex or age—in such cases, there can be no question but that, within certain limits, it would be right to invoke the aid and authority of the law. The limits must be determined by the nature of the occasion which calls for the law's interference—the principle being that the law must not undertake more, nor proceed further, than is required for the remedy of the evil or the removal of the mischief.

37. Rights must be religiously respected wherever they exist, and it is the duty of the public authority to prevent and to punish injury, and to protect every one in the possession of his own. Still, when there is question of defending the rights of individuals, the poor and badly off have a claim to especial consideration. The richer class have many ways of shielding themselves, and stand less in need of help from the State; whereas the mass of the poor have no resources of their own to fall back upon, and must chiefly depend upon the assistance of the State. And it is for this reason that wage-earners, since they mostly belong in the mass of the needy, should be specially cared for and protected by the government.

38. Here, however, it is expedient to bring under special notice certain matters of moment. First of all, there is the duty of safe-guarding private property by legal enactment and protection. Most of all it is essential, where the passion of greed is so strong, to keep the populace within the line of duty; for, if all may justly strive to better their condition, neither justice nor the common good allows any individual to seize upon that which belongs to another, or, under the futile and shallow pretext of equality, to lay violent hands on other people's possessions. Most true it is that by far the larger part of the workers prefer to better themselves by honest labor rather than by doing any wrong to others. But there are not a few who are imbued with evil principles and eager for revolutionary change, whose main purpose is to

stir up disorder and incite their fellows to acts of violence. The authority of the law should intervene to put restraint upon such firebrands, to save the working classes from being led astray by their maneuvers, and to protect lawful owners from spoliation.

39. When work people have recourse to a strike and become voluntarily idle, it is frequently because the hours of labor are too long, or the work too hard, or because they consider their wages insufficient. The grave inconvenience of this not uncommon occurrence should be obviated by public remedial measures; for such paralysing of labor not only affects the masters and their work people alike, but is extremely injurious to trade and to the general interests of the public; moreover, on such occasions, violence and disorder are generally not far distant, and thus it frequently happens that the public peace is imperiled. The laws should forestall and prevent such troubles from arising; they should lend their influence and authority to the removal in good time of the causes which lead to conflicts between employers and employed.

40. The working man, too, has interests in which he should be protected by the State; and first of all, there are the interests of his soul. Life on earth, however good and desirable in itself, is not the final purpose for which man is created; it is only the way and the means to that attainment of truth and that love of goodness in which the full life of the soul consists. It is the soul which is made after the image and likeness of God; it is in the soul that the sovereignty resides in virtue whereof man is commanded to rule the creatures below him and to use all the earth and the ocean for his profit and advantage. "Fill the earth and subdue it; and rule over the fishes of the sea, and the fowls of the air, and all living creatures that move upon the earth."[29] In this respect all men are equal; there is here no difference between rich and poor, master and servant, ruler and ruled, "for the same is Lord over all."[30] No man may with impunity outrage that human dignity which God Himself treats with great reverence, nor stand in the way of that higher life which is the preparation of the eternal life of heaven. Nay, more; no man has in this matter power over himself. To consent to any treatment which is calculated to defeat the end and purpose of his being is

beyond his right; he cannot give up his soul to servitude, for it is not man's own rights which are here in question, but the rights of God, the most sacred and inviolable of rights.

41. From this follows the obligation of the cessation from work and labor on Sundays and certain holy days. The rest from labor is not to be understood as mere giving way to idleness; much less must it be an occasion for spending money and for vicious indulgence, as many would have it to be; but it should be rest from labor, hallowed by religion. Rest (combined with religious observances) disposes man to forget for a while the business of his everyday life, to turn his thoughts to things heavenly, and to the worship which he so strictly owes to the eternal Godhead. It is this, above all, which is the reason and motive of Sunday rest; a rest sanctioned by God's great law of the Ancient Covenant—"Remember thou keep holy the Sabbath day,"[31] and taught to the world by His own mysterious "rest" after the creation of man: "He rested on the seventh day from all His work which He had done."[32]

42. If we turn not to things external and material, the first thing of all to secure is to save unfortunate working people from the cruelty of men of greed, who use human beings as mere instruments for money-making. It is neither just nor human so to grind men down with excessive labor as to stupefy their minds and wear out their bodies. Man's powers, like his general nature, are limited, and beyond these limits he cannot go. His strength is developed and increased by use and exercise, but only on condition of due intermission and proper rest. Daily labor, therefore, should be so regulated as not to be protracted over longer hours than strength admits. How many and how long the intervals of rest should be must depend on the nature of the work, on circumstances of time and place, and on the health and strength of the workman. Those who work in mines and quarries, and extract coal, stone and metals from the bowels of the earth, should have shorter hours in proportion as their labor is more severe and trying to health. Then, again, the season of the year should be taken into account; for not unfrequently a kind of labor is easy at one time which at another is intolerable

or exceedingly difficult. Finally, work which is quite suitable for a strong man cannot rightly be required from a woman or a child. And, in regard to children, great care should be taken not to place them in workshops and factories until their bodies and minds are sufficiently developed. For, just as very rough weather destroys the buds of spring, so does too early an experience of life's hard toil blight the young promise of a child's faculties, and render any true education impossible. Women, again, are not suited for certain occupations; a woman is by nature fitted for home-work, and it is that which is best adapted at once to preserve her modesty and to promote the good bringing-up of children and the well-being of the family. As a general principle it may be laid down that a workman ought to have leisure and rest proportionate to the wear and tear of his strength, for waste of strength must be repaired by cessation from hard work.

In all agreements between masters and work people there is always the condition expressed or understood that there should be allowed proper rest for soul and body. To agree in any other sense would be against what is right and just; for it can never be just or right to require on the one side, or to promise on the other, the giving up of those duties which a man owes to his God and to himself.

43. We now approach a subject of great importance, and one in respect of which, if extremes are to be avoided, right notions are absolutely necessary. Wages, as we are told, are regulated by free consent, and therefore the employer, when he pays what was agreed upon, has done his part and seemingly is not called upon to do anything beyond. The only way, it is said, in which injustice might occur would be if the master refused to pay the whole of the wages, or if the workman should not complete the work undertaken; in such cases the public authority should intervene, to see that each obtains his due, but not under any other circumstances.

44. To this kind of argument a fair-minded man will not easily or entirely assent; it is not complete, for there are important considerations which it leaves out of account altogether. To labor is to exert oneself for the sake of procuring what is necessary for the various purposes of life, and chief of all for self-preservation.

"In the sweat of thy face thou shalt eat bread."[33] Hence, a man's labor necessarily bears two notes or characters. First of all, it is *personal*, inasmuch as the force which acts is bound up with the personality and is the exclusive property of him who acts, and, further, was given to him for his advantage. Secondly, man's labor is *necessary*; for without the result of labor a man cannot live, and self-preservation is a law of nature, which it is wrong to disobey. Now, were we to consider labor merely in so far as it is personal, doubtless it would be within the workman's right to accept any rate of wages whatsoever; for in the same way as he is free to work or not, so is he free to accept a small wage or even none at all. But our conclusion must be very different if, together with the personal element in a man's work, we consider the fact that work is also necessary for him to live: these two aspects of his work are separable in thought, but not in reality. The preservation of life is the bounden duty of one and all, and to be wanting therein is a crime. It necessarily follows that each one has a natural right to procure what is required in order to live, and the poor can procure that in no other way than by what they can earn through their work.

45. Let the working man and the employer make free agreements, and in particular let them agree freely as to the wages; nevertheless, there underlies a dictate of natural justice more imperious and ancient than any bargain between man and man, namely, that wages ought not to be insufficient to support a frugal and well-behaved wage-earner. If through necessity or fear of a worse evil the workman accept harder conditions because an employer or contractor will afford him no better, he is made the victim of force and injustice. In these and similar questions, however—such as, for example, the hours of labor in different trades, the sanitary precautions to be observed in factories and workshops, etc.—in order to supersede undue interference on the part of the State, especially as circumstances, times, and localities differ so widely, it is advisable that recourse be had to societies or boards such as We shall mention presently, or to some other mode of safeguarding the interests of the wage-earners; the State being appealed to, should circumstances require, for its sanction and protection.

46. If a workman's wages be sufficient to enable him comfortably to support himself, his wife, and his children, he will find it easy, if he be a sensible man, to practice thrift, and he will not fail, by cutting down expenses, to put by some little savings and thus secure a modest source of income. Nature itself would urge him to this. We have seen that this great labor question cannot be solved save by assuming as a principle that private ownership must be held sacred and inviolable. The law, therefore, should favor ownership, and its policy should be to induce as many as possible of the people to become owners.

47. Many excellent results will follow from this; and, first of all, property will certainly become more equitably divided. For, the result of civil change and revolution has been to divide cities into two classes separated by a wide chasm. On the one side there is the party which holds power because it holds wealth; which has in its grasp the whole of labor and trade; which manipulates for its own benefit and its own purposes all the sources of supply, and which is not without influence even in the administration of the commonwealth. On the other side there is the needy and powerless multitude, sick and sore in spirit and ever ready for disturbance. If working people can be encouraged to look forward to obtaining a share in the land, the consequence will be that the gulf between vast wealth and sheer poverty will be bridged over, and the respective classes will be brought nearer to one another. A further consequence will result in the great abundance of the fruits of the earth. Men always work harder and more readily when they work on that which belongs to them; nay, they learn to love the very soil that yields in response to the labor of their hands, not only food to eat, but an abundance of good things for themselves and those that are dear to them. That such a spirit of willing labor would add to the produce of the earth and to the wealth of the community is self-evident. And a third advantage would spring from this: men would cling to the country in which they were born, for no one would exchange his country for a foreign land if his own afforded him the means of living a decent and happy life. These three important benefits, however, can be reckoned on only provided that a man's means be not drained and exhausted by excessive taxation. The right to possess private

property is derived from nature, not from man; and the State has the right to control its use in the interests of the public good alone, but by no means to absorb it altogether. The State would therefore be unjust and cruel if under the name of taxation it were to deprive the private owner of more than is fair.

48. In the last place, employers and workmen may of themselves effect much, in the matter We are treating, by means of such associations and organizations as afford opportune aid to those who are in distress, and which draw the two classes more closely together. Among these may be enumerated societies for mutual help; various benevolent foundations established by private persons to provide for the workman, and for his widow or his orphans, in case of sudden calamity, in sickness, and in the event of death; and institutions for the welfare of boys and girls, young people, and those more advanced in years.

49. The most important of all are workingmen's unions, for these virtually include all the rest. History attests what excellent results were brought about by the artificers' guilds of olden times. They were the means of affording not only many advantages to the workmen, but in no small degree of promoting the advancement of art, as numerous monuments remain to bear witness. Such unions should be suited to the requirements of this our age—an age of wider education, of different habits, and of far more numerous requirements in daily life. It is gratifying to know that there are actually in existence not a few associations of this nature, consisting either of workmen alone, or of workmen and employers together, but it were greatly to be desired that they should become more numerous and more efficient. We have spoken of them more than once, yet it will be well to explain here how notably they are needed, to show that they exist of their own right, and what should be their organization and their mode of action.

50. The consciousness of his own weakness urges man to call in aid from without. We read in the pages of holy Writ: "It is better that two should be together than one; for they have the advantage of their society. If one fall he shall be supported by the other. Woe to him that is alone, for when he falleth he hath none to lift him up."[34] And further: "A brother that is helped

by his brother is like a strong city."[35] It is this natural impulse which binds men together in civil society; and it is likewise this which leads them to join together in associations which are, it is true, lesser and not independent societies, but, nevertheless, real societies.

51. These lesser societies and the larger society differ in many respects, because their immediate purpose and aim are different. Civil society exists for the common good, and hence is concerned with the interests of all in general, albeit with individual interests also in their due place and degree. It is therefore called a *public* society, because by its agency, as St. Thomas of Aquinas says, "Men establish relations in common with one another in the setting up of a commonwealth."[36] But societies which are formed in the bosom of the commonwealth are styled *private*, and rightly so, since their immediate purpose is the private advantage of the associates. "Now, a private society," says St. Thomas again, "is one which is formed for the purpose of carrying out private objects; as when two or three enter into partnership with the view of trading in common."[37] Private societies, then, although they exist within the body politic, and are severally part of the commonwealth, cannot nevertheless be absolutely, and as such, prohibited by public authority. For, to enter into a "society" of this kind is the natural right of man; and the State has for its office to protect natural rights, not to destroy them; and, if it forbid its citizens to form associations, it contradicts the very principle of its own existence, for both they and it exist in virtue of the like principle, namely, the natural tendency of man to dwell in society.

52. There are occasions, doubtless, when it is fitting that the law should intervene to prevent certain associations, as when men join together for purposes which are evidently bad, unlawful, or dangerous to the State. In such cases, public authority may justly forbid the formation of such associations, and may dissolve them if they already exist. But every precaution should be taken not to violate the rights of individuals and not to impose unreasonable regulations under pretense of public benefit. For laws only bind when they are in accordance with right reason, and, hence, with the eternal law of God.[38]

53. And here we are reminded of the confraternities, societies, and religious orders which have arisen by the Church's authority and the piety of Christian men. The annals of every nation down to our own days bear witness to what they have accomplished for the human race. It is indisputable that on grounds of reason alone such associations, being perfectly blameless in their objects, possess the sanction of the law of nature. In their religious aspect they claim rightly to be responsible to the Church alone. The rulers of the State accordingly have no rights over them, nor can they claim any share in their control; on the contrary, it is the duty of the State to respect and cherish them, and, if need be, to defend them from attack. It is notorious that a very different course has been followed, more especially in our own times. In many places the State authorities have laid violent hands on these communities, and committed manifold injustice against them; it has placed them under control of the civil law, taken away their rights as corporate bodies, and despoiled them of their property, in such property the Church had her rights, each member of the body had his or her rights, and there were also the rights of those who had founded or endowed these communities for a definite purpose, and, furthermore, of those for whose benefit and assistance they had their being. Therefore We cannot refrain from complaining of such spoliation as unjust and fraught with evil results; and with all the more reason do We complain because, at the very time when the law proclaims that association is free to all, We see that Catholic societies, however peaceful and useful, are hampered in every way, whereas the utmost liberty is conceded to individuals whose purposes are at once hurtful to religion and dangerous to the commonwealth.

54. Associations of every kind, and especially those of working men, are now far more common than heretofore. As regards many of these there is no need at present to inquire whence they spring, what are their objects, or what the means they employ. Now, there is a good deal of evidence in favor of the opinion that many of these societies are in the hands of secret leaders, and are managed on principles ill-according with Christianity and the public well-being; and that they do their utmost to get within their grasp the whole field of labor, and force working men either

to join them or to starve. Under these circumstances Christian working men must do one of two things: either join associations in which their religion will be exposed to peril, or form associations among themselves and unite their forces so as to shake off courageously the yoke of so unrighteous and intolerable an oppression. No one who does not wish to expose man's chief good to extreme risk will for a moment hesitate to say that the second alternative should by all means be adopted.

55. Those Catholics are worthy of all praise—and they are not a few—who, understanding what the times require, have striven, by various undertakings and endeavors, to better the condition of the working class by rightful means. They have taken up the cause of the working man, and have spared no efforts to better the condition both of families and individuals; to infuse a spirit of equity into the mutual relations of employers and employed; to keep before the eyes of both classes the precepts of duty and the laws of the Gospel—that Gospel which, by inculcating self-restraint, keeps men within the bounds of moderation, and tends to establish harmony among the divergent interests and the various classes which compose the body politic. It is with such ends in view that we see men of eminence, meeting together for discussion, for the promotion of concerted action, and for practical work. Others, again, strive to unite working men of various grades into associations, help them with their advice and means, and enable them to obtain fitting and profitable employment. The bishops, on their part, bestow their ready good-will and support; and with their approval and guidance many members of the clergy, both secular and regular, labor assiduously in behalf of the spiritual interest of the members of such associations. And there are not wanting Catholics blessed with affluence, who have, as it were, cast in their lot with the wage-earners, and who have spent large sums in founding and widely spreading benefit and insurance societies, by means of which the working man may without difficulty acquire through his labor not only many present advantages, but also the certainty of honorable support in days to come. How greatly such manifold and earnest activity has benefited the community at large is too well known to require Us to dwell upon it. We find

therein grounds for most cheering hope in the future, provided always that the associations We have described continue to grow and spread, and are well and wisely administered. The State should watch over these societies of citizens banded together in accordance with their rights, but it should not thrust itself into their peculiar concerns and their organization, for things move and live by the spirit inspiring them, and may be killed by the rough grasp of a hand from without.

56. In order that an association may be carried on with unity of purpose and harmony of action, its administration and government should be firm and wise. All such societies, being free to exist, have the further right to adopt such rules and organization as may best conduce to the attainment of their respective objects. We do not judge it possible to enter into minute particulars touching the subject of organization; this must depend on national character, on practice and experience, on the nature and aim of the work to be done, on the scope of the various trades and employments, and on other circumstances of fact and of time—all of which should be carefully considered.

57. To sum up, then, We may lay it down as a general and lasting law that working men's associations should be so organized and governed as to furnish the best and most suitable means for attaining what is aimed at, that is to say, for helping each individual member to better his condition to the utmost in body, soul, and property. It is clear that they must pay special and chief attention to the duties of religion and morality, and that social betterment should have this chiefly in view; otherwise they would lose wholly their special character, and end by becoming little better than those societies which take no account whatever of religion. What advantage can it be to a working man to obtain by means of a society material well-being, if he endangers his soul for lack of spiritual food? "What doth it profit a man, if he gain the whole world and suffer the loss of his soul?"[39] This, as our Lord teaches, is the mark or character that distinguishes the Christian from the heathen. "After all these things do the heathen seek ... Seek ye first the Kingdom of God and His justice: and all these things shall be added unto you."[40] Let our associations, then, look first and before all things

to God; let religious instruction have therein the foremost place, each one being carefully taught what is his duty to God, what he has to believe, what to hope for, and how he is to work out his salvation; and let all be warned and strengthened with special care against wrong principles and false teaching. Let the working man be urged and led to the worship of God, to the earnest practice of religion, and, among other things, to the keeping holy of Sundays and holy days. Let him learn to reverence and love holy Church, the common Mother of us all; and hence to obey the precepts of the Church, and to frequent the sacraments, since they are the means ordained by God for obtaining forgiveness of sin and for leading a holy life.

58. The foundations of the organization being thus laid in religion, We next proceed to make clear the relations of the members one to another, in order that they may live together in concord and go forward prosperously and with good results. The offices and charges of the society should be apportioned for the good of the society itself, and in such mode that difference in degree or standing should not interfere with unanimity and good-will. It is most important that office-bearers be appointed with due prudence and discretion, and each one's charge carefully mapped out, in order that no members may suffer harm. The common funds must be administered with strict honesty, in such a way that a member may receive assistance in proportion to his necessities. The rights and duties of the employers, as compared with the rights and duties of the employed, ought to be the subject of careful consideration. Should it happen that either a master or a workman believes himself injured, nothing would be more desirable than that a committee should be appointed, composed of reliable and capable members of the association, whose duty would be, conformably with the rules of the association, to settle the dispute. Among the several purposes of a society, one should be to try to arrange for a continuous supply of work at all times and seasons; as well as to create a fund out of which the members may be effectually helped in their needs, not only in the cases of accident, but also in sickness, old age, and distress.

59. Such rules and regulations, if willingly obeyed by all, will sufficiently ensure the well being of the less well-to-do; whilst such mutual associations among Catholics are certain to be productive in no small degree of prosperity to the State. It is not rash to conjecture the future from the past. Age gives way to age, but the events of one century are wonderfully like those of another, for they are directed by the providence of God, who overrules the course of history in accordance with His purposes in creating the race of man. We are told that it was cast as a reproach on the Christians in the early ages of the Church that the greater number among them had to live by begging or by labor. Yet, destitute though they were of wealth and influence, they ended by winning over to their side the favor of the rich and the good-will of the powerful. They showed themselves industrious, hard-working, assiduous, and peaceful, ruled by justice, and, above all, bound together in brotherly love. In presence of such mode of life and such example, prejudice gave way, the tongue of malevolence was silenced, and the lying legends of ancient superstition little by little yielded to Christian truth.

60. At the time being, the condition of the working classes is the pressing question of the hour, and nothing can be of higher interest to all classes of the State than that it should be rightly and reasonably settled. But it will be easy for Christian working men to solve it aright if they will form associations, choose wise guides, and follow on the path which with so much advantage to themselves and the common weal was trodden by their fathers before them. Prejudice, it is true, is mighty, and so is the greed of money; but if the sense of what is just and rightful be not deliberately stifled, their fellow citizens are sure to be won over to a kindly feeling towards men whom they see to be in earnest as regards their work and who prefer so unmistakably right dealing to mere lucre, and the sacredness of duty to every other consideration.

61. And further great advantage would result from the state of things We are describing; there would exist so much more ground for hope, and likelihood, even, of recalling to a sense of their duty those working men who have either given up their faith altogether, or whose lives are at variance with its precepts.

Such men feel in most cases that they have been fooled by empty promises and deceived by false pretexts. They cannot but perceive that their grasping employers too often treat them with great inhumanity and hardly care for them outside the profit their labor brings; and if they belong to any union, it is probably one in which there exists, instead of charity and love, that intestine strife which ever accompanies poverty when unresigned and unsustained by religion. Broken in spirit and worn down in body, how many of them would gladly free themselves from such galling bondage! But human respect, or the dread of starvation, makes them tremble to take the step. To such as these Catholic associations are of incalculable service, by helping them out of their difficulties, inviting them to companionship and receiving the returning wanderers to a haven where they may securely find repose.

62. We have now laid before you, venerable brethren, both who are the persons and what are the means whereby this most arduous question must be solved. Every one should put his hand to the work which falls to his share, and that at once and straightway, lest the evil which is already so great become through delay absolutely beyond remedy. Those who rule the commonwealths should avail themselves of the laws and institutions of the country; masters and wealthy owners must be mindful of their duty; the working class, whose interests are at stake, should make every lawful and proper effort; and since religion alone, as We said at the beginning, can avail to destroy the evil at its root, all men should rest persuaded that the main thing needful is to re-establish Christian morals, apart from which all the plans and devices of the wisest will prove of little avail.

63. In regard to the Church, her co-operation will never be found lacking, be the time or the occasion what it may; and she will intervene with all the greater effect in proportion as her liberty of action is the more unfettered. Let this be carefully taken to heart by those whose office it is to safeguard the public welfare. Every minister of holy religion must bring to the struggle the full energy of his mind and all his power of endurance. Moved by your authority, venerable brethren, and quickened by your example, they should never cease to urge upon men of every class,

upon the high-placed as well as the lowly, the Gospel doctrines of Christian life; by every means in their power they must strive to secure the good of the people; and above all must earnestly cherish in themselves, and try to arouse in others, charity, the mistress and the queen of virtues. For, the happy results we all long for must be chiefly brought about by the plenteous outpouring of charity; of that true Christian charity which is the fulfilling of the whole Gospel law, which is always ready to sacrifice itself for others' sake, and is man's surest antidote against worldly pride and immoderate love of self; that charity whose office is described and whose Godlike features are outlined by the Apostle St. Paul in these words: "Charity is patient, is kind, ... seeketh not her own, ... suffereth all things, ... endureth all things."[41]

64. On each of you, venerable brethren, and on your clergy and people, as an earnest of God's mercy and a mark of Our affection, we lovingly in the Lord bestow the apostolic benediction.

Given at St. Peter's in Rome, the fifteenth day of May, 1891, the fourteenth year of Our pontificate.

LEO XIII, *Pope.*

Notes

1. [Note by Étienne Gilson:] The title sometimes given to this encyclical, *On the Condition of the Working Classes*, is therefore perfectly justified. A few lines after this sentence, the Pope gives a more comprehensive definition of the subject of *Rerum Novarum*. We are using it as a title.

2. Deut. 5:21.

3. Gen. 1:28.

4. *Summa theologiae*, IIa-IIae, q. x, art. 12, Answer.

5. Gen. 3:17.

6. James 5:4.

7. 2 Tim. 2:12.

8. 2 Cor. 4:17.

9. Matt. 19:23–24.

10. Luke 6:24–25.

11. *Summa theologiae*, IIa-IIae, q. lxvi, art. 2, Answer.

12. Ibid.

13. Ibid., q. xxxii, a. 6, Answer.

14. Luke 11:41.

15. Acts 20:35.

16. Matt. 25:40.

17. *Hom. in Evang.*, 9, n. 7 (PL 76, 1109B).

18. 2 Cor. 8:9.

19. Mark 6:3.

20. Matt. 5:3.

21. Matt. 11:28.

22. Rom. 8:17.

23. 1 Tim. 6:10.

24. Acts 4:34.

25. *Apologia secunda*, 39, (*Apologeticus*, cap. 39; PL 1, 533A).

26. See above, pp. 161–184. [This is Gilson's reference to the text of Leo XIII, encyclical letter *Immortale Dei* (November 1, 1885), as it appears in his edition.]

27. *Summa theologiae*, IIa-IIae, q. lxi, art. 1, ad 2m.

28. Thomas Aquinas, *On the Governance of Rulers*, 1, 15 (*Opera omnia*, ed. Vives, Vol. 27, p. 356).

29. Gen. 1:28.

30. Rom. 10:12.

31. Exod. 20:8.

32. Gen. 2:2.

33. Gen. 3:19.

34. Eccle. 4:9–10.

35. Prov. 18:19.

36. *Contra impugnantes Dei cultum et religionem*, Part 2, ch. 8 (*Opera omnia*, ed. Vives, Vol. 29, p. 16).

37. Ibid.

38. "Human law is law only by virtue of its accordance with right reason; and thus it is manifest that it flows from the eternal law. And in so far as it deviates from right reason it is called an unjust law; in such case it is no law at all, but rather a species of violence." Thomas Aquinas, *Summa theologiae*, Ia-IIae, q. xciii, art. 3, ad 2m.

39. Matt. 16:26.

40. Matt. 6:32–33.

41. 1 Cor. 13:4–7.

THE SOCIAL QUESTION
AND THE CHRISTIAN RELIGION

Text Introduction

This speech by Abraham Kuyper was given as the opening address at the Christian Social Congress, which met in Amsterdam on November 9–12, 1891. This new translation has been carefully compared at every point with the first English translation by Dirk Jellema, published as *Christianity and the Class Struggle* (Grand Rapids: Piet Hein Publishers, 1950), and the second edited by James W. Skillen, published as *The Problem of Poverty* (Grand Rapids: Baker, 1991; repr., Sioux Center, IA: Dordt College Press, 2011). The four divisions and the subheadings that were added to the Skillen edition have also been adopted. All references, unless indicated otherwise by brackets or identified as editor's notes, are Kuyper's; most of them are here translated in full for the first time. Kuyper's references have been conformed to modern style conventions where possible.

Source: Kuyper, Abraham. *Het Sociale Vraagstuk en de Christelijke Religie: Rede bij de opening van het Sociaal Congres op 9 November 1891 gehouden.* Amsterdam: J. A. Wormser, 1891. Translated by Harry Van Dyke. Annotations by Jordan J. Ballor and Harry Van Dyke.

The Social Question
and the Christian Religion

ABRAHAM KUYPER

I. Facing the Reality of Poverty

I think I will act in accordance with your wishes if right at the outset, in this opening address, I define the purpose of our first congress as modestly as possible. Not for a moment should the idea take hold that we mean to emulate one of those impressive assemblies where specialists from every country in Europe come together to display their wealth of knowledge and show off their brilliant talents. One unfortunate result of the state's monopoly on higher education in our country is that we have not as yet produced any specialists[1]; none of us at this congress stands out as an authority on economics, for example. And unless my senses deceive me, you have not come here to cross swords with the opposition in a public tournament, but rather to talk among ourselves as brothers united in the name of Jesus for the purpose of having a serious discussion of this question: What should we be doing as confessors of Christ about the social needs of our time?

In other countries, too, people who profess Jesus have increasingly realized that action is needed. Think of the action of the Christian Social Workers' Party [*Christlichsoziale Arbeiterspartei*] in the circle around Count Waldersee in Berlin,[2] or the Christian Socialists, inspired by Maurice and Kingsley, who have joined forces in London under Rev. Headlam,[3] or the Christian Society of Social Economics [*Société chrétienne pour économie sociale*] of Switzerland, organized two years ago in Geneva.[4] And speaking of Christianity in the broadest sense, think of what has been done toward a solution of the social question from the side of Catholics[5] by such capable intellectuals as Le Play[6] and Von Ketteler,[7] by a whole series of significant congresses in Germany, France, and Belgium; and most recently by Leo XIII in his encyclical.[8]

We Have Been Too Slow to Act

Our own entry, therefore, does not come too early but too late. We lag behind others when we could have been in the vanguard. After all, before a single voice had been raised by Christians outside our borders, Willem Bilderdijk, Isaac da Costa, and Willem Groen van Prinsterer had already called our attention to the social problem.[9] As early as 1825 Bilderdijk addressed the lower classes in this vein:

> You sigh and languish in poverty and decay,
> While luxury feasts on the fruit of your hands.

And in the face of this problem he parodied the false theory of philanthropy when he introduced a classical liberal as saying:

> The land is weighted down with paupers:
> To a work camp with them! Good riddance.
> They're only rascals on relief that we pity,
> but even the deserving poor cost far too much.
> The poor are hungry, sure; but do they have a job?
> What use are they when jobs for them are lacking?

By contrast, Bilderdijk put his finger on the sore spot by calling Christians to repentance in the opening lines of his volume of biting verse:

> Whenever a people is fated to perish in sin,
> in the church the disease of the soul will begin.[10]

Some fifteen years later, Da Costa lashed out with equal relentlessness at the plutocracy—the "rule of money," as he called it. He pictured the social problem—then imminent, today all too real—in the following contrast:

Here, disproportionate luxury, outwardly healthy,
glowing with youth, but inwardly scorched,
destroying the sap of life, as like a cancer,
undoing the balance between the classes ...
There, muttering at toil that gives no bread; free men
weighed down by yokes, at sites where walls
blaze night and day with heat, and cityscapes grow black
from everlasting smoke, and souls are choked by fumes.[11]

When Da Costa penned this prophecy he was not parroting socialism but speaking a quarter century before Karl Marx founded his International in London in 1864. And in 1853 Groen van Prinsterer frightened the members of parliament with his brusque declaration: "As for the ideas of socialism, one should be mindful of the wretched condition of the lower classes, and especially of the harm that the higher classes, through their moral corruption and false science, have brought about among the common people." Groen declared that in socialism "truth is mingled with error, which gives it power," and he recognized that "we must strive to improve material conditions too, the unjustness of which redoubles the influence of the socialist error."[12] He called upon his fellow Christians to extinguish the fire when he wrote that "socialism finds its source in the French Revolution and," like the Revolution, "can only be vanquished by Christianity."[13]

Thus we have been declared to be in default. And that not only by our God-given leaders, but just as strongly by the socialists. They have never stopped appealing to Christ for their utopias. They constantly hold before us solemn Bible texts. In fact, they feel the connection between the social needs and the Christian religion so strongly that they have not hesitated to present Christ himself as the great prophet of socialism and to exclaim: "There can be no talk of the failure of the Christian work of emancipation: a mere two thousand years lie between the beginning and the conclusion of the work initiated by Christ."[14]

Accordingly, a liberal of the old school, Alfred Naquet, is worried that socialism might pave the way for new triumphs for Christianity, and he reproaches socialists precisely for furthering the cause of religion despite their hatred of it. "You are doing the work of religion," he exclaims, "when you put in the foreground exactly those problems whose solution closely involves Christianity."[15] This is an unintentional yet telling tribute to the influence that Christianity can exercise in helping solve the social question—an influence that comes out even more beautifully in these rich words of Fichte:

> Christianity conceals within its womb a much greater treasure for the renewal of life than one suspects. Thus far it has applied its strength only to *individuals* and only indirectly to the state. But anyone, believer or unbeliever, who has been in a position to notice Christianity's hidden driving force must grant that it could apply marvelous organizational strength also *to society*. Once this strength breaks to the surface, the Religion of the Cross will shine before the whole world in all the profoundness of its ideas and all the wealth of blessing it brings.[16]

But enough citations, Gentlemen[17]—more than enough—to convince you that one simply cannot deny the intimate connection between the social question and the Christian religion. We feel ashamed that this conviction has not been stronger among us, or at any rate has not roused us to action much earlier. We are humbly penitent in the face of such crying need. Why has it taken so long for us to move into action in the name of Jesus?

Do you protest that this obvious truth need not be argued in a gathering such as this? I take your protest to be prompted by a spirit of self-reproach, not pride. In the face of the enormous needs of our time, needs which at every point are connected to the very core of error and sin, how could we possibly fail to look to *Christus Consolator*, who never ceases to call out with divine compassion also to our deeply troubled times: "Come unto me, richest century that ever was, yet so deadly weary and heavy, and I will give you rest."

The Connection between Christianity and the Problem of Poverty

Let me not spend another word on the reality of this connection. The very presupposition of this congress is that we acknowledge it. But what you do expect of me—and, with your indulgence, what I shall endeavor to offer—is to lay bare the threads by which these two phenomena (on the one hand the Christian religion and on the other the social question) are intimately connected. To be convinced that this connection is real is not enough: it must also become concrete, so that it can raise our consciousness.[18]

As my point of departure I shall take a contrast that is plain for all to see. I mean the contrast between nature as it exists independent of our will, and our human art that acts on nature.[19] The entire social question, we should realize, arises from the connection between human life and the material world that surrounds us. Now in human life, as well as in the material world, there is on the one hand a power beyond our reach that we commonly call *nature*, and on the other there is a power originating in the human will that we may refer to simply as *art*. Our human nature is placed in the nature that surrounds us, not in order to leave nature as it is, but to work on nature instinctively and irrepressibly, by means of art, to improve and perfect it. An example is the stud farm for creating thoroughbreds. Another is the skill of the florist who does not just gather bouquets of wild flowers but multiplies and refines varieties by mingling seeds. Men heat water to make steam and cut stone to produce diamonds. They harness rushing streams that split the mountains by guiding them into safer channels, to use the water for shipping and irrigation. In short, human art acts on every area of nature not to destroy it—much less to erect a mechanical structure alongside it—but rather to unlock nature's hidden strength, or else to tame its wild force. God's ordinances require this. While still in Paradise, man was given the mandate "to preserve and cultivate" the material world.[20] It was created for man to improve and perfect it. "All creatures," our Confession states so beautifully, were made "for the service of mankind, to the end that man may serve his God."[21]

It follows that this applies equally to human life, both in its personal and social aspects. We neglect our duty if we allow our inner nature to run its course unrestrained and fail to come to its aid to ennoble it through the holy art of "watching, praying, and struggling."[22] Shame on fathers and mothers who let their children grow up naturally without acting upon nature through nurture and education. And it is nothing but primitive barbarism to abandon society to the course of nature without human intervention. The art of politics, too, taken in the higher sense of statecraft, intervenes so that society may develop into a community; and so that social life, both by itself and in its relation to the material world, may be ennobled.[23]

If in the course of history man had not made mistakes or fallen into error, and no crime or egoism had disrupted this natural development, human society would have run its course in peace and advanced undisturbed toward an ever greater state of happiness. Alas, humankind did not live in such a desirable state. To be sure, among virtually all peoples human instinct has prompted men to acknowledge certain indispensable standards for any human society, and from ancient times men of genius and courage have made many felicitous contributions in this area. But as soon as the need arose for a more elaborate ordering of the complex phenomenon we call human society, action after action was misdirected, both by those who set the tone in society and by those who held the reins of power.

Human Error and Sin

In both instances the series of misdirected actions was invariably caused either by error or by sin. The cause was error whenever people were ignorant of the essence of human nature and its social attributes, and unaware of the laws governing society and the production, distribution, and use of material goods. But the cause was also—and just as much—sin. Owing to men's greed or hunger for power, sin disrupted or thwarted a healthy growth of society, sometimes by violence, and then again by false practices and unjust laws. Occasionally it caused a very unhealthy development to fester for centuries. As time went on, error and sin joined forces to enthrone false principles that violated human nature and to erect out of these false principles whole systems that gave injustice a semblance of justice and stamped as normal what was actually in conflict with the demands of life.[24]

This reckless play with human society was carried on among all peoples in every age. It was carried on in private life by intellectuals and property owners, and before long, under their inspiration and just as recklessly, by governments. For while it is perfectly true that the social question in the narrower sense is discussed only very intermittently, with the result that many people are under the delusion that government intervention in social problems is a novelty of our own time, yet actually there has never been any country in the world where the government did not in various ways control both the course of social life and its relationship to material wealth. Governments have done so by means of all kinds of rules in civil law; they have done so through commercial codes, indirectly also through constitutional law and criminal law. In regard to material wealth, governments have intervened by means of inheritance law, the system of taxation, import and export duties, regulations governing real estate, agriculture, colonial administration, coinage, and so much more. It has never been possible in any developed country to speak of a free, entirely instinctual development of society; human art has everywhere taken in hand the development of natural forces and relationships. But while we must gratefully acknowledge that this intervention by human art has in general brought us from a barbaric situation to a well-ordered society—indeed, while we must concede that the continuous unfolding of society reinforces our belief in an overriding rule of Providence—yet we cannot for a moment doubt that this government intervention, which often proceeded from untrue principles, in every age has made conditions unsound when they could have been sound. It has in many ways poisoned our relationships and brought about untold misery, even as the end of government should be the happiness and dignity of its people.[25]

The inequality among men, which cannot be undone, gave the stronger an ascendancy over the weaker, as though we were not a human society but a herd of animals where the rule holds that the stronger animals devour the weaker ones. The stronger almost always managed to bend every custom and government ordinance in such a way that they stood to gain and the weaker lost out. They did not sink their teeth into each other's flesh, like cannibals, but the powerful ground down the weak with a weapon against which there was no defense. And where governments as servants of God still protected the weak, the more powerful class of society soon learned how to exert such a preponderant influence on politics that governmental authority, which should have protected the weak, became a weapon against them.[26] This was not because the stronger man was more evil in his heart than the weaker man, since no sooner did a member of the lower class rise to the top than he in turn took part just as harshly—if not more harshly—in the wicked oppression of members of his former class. No, the cause of the evil lay in this: that man was cut off from his eternal destiny and not honored as created in the image of God. Nor did men reckon with the majesty of the Lord, who alone by his grace is mighty to bridle a generation sunk in sin.

This unjust situation arose already in ancient times, of which the Preacher complains so movingly: "Again I saw all the oppressions that are done under the sun. And behold, the tears of the oppressed, and they had no one to comfort them! On the side of their oppressors there was power, and there was no one to comfort them" (Eccl 4:1).[27] Think of situations like the one where Naboth was murdered so that Jezebel could add his field to the royal park of Ahab [see 1 Kgs 21:1–16]. Or if you will, situations that were forever stigmatized by our Lord in the parable of the rich man and poor Lazarus [see Luke 16:19–31], and situations against which James flung his apostolic anathema when he wrote:

> Come now, you rich, weep and howl for the miseries that are coming upon you. Behold, the wages of the laborers who mowed your fields, which you kept back by fraud, are crying out against you, and the cries of the harvesters have reached the ears of the Lord of hosts. (Jas 5:1,4)[28]

II. Jesus and the Social Question

Now is it conceivable, friends, that the Christian religion, when it came into the world, did not take a stand against so criminal a state of affairs? I am sure you are aware how at the time these social conditions, worse even than those that today keep Europe and America in a state of tension, foretold the imminent fall of the Roman Empire. A truly Asiatic despotism in almost every colony of Rome maintained a system of exploitation and extortion against which great orators like Cicero more than once raised their voice in vain. In those days, as in our day, the balance between classes was gone: brazen luxury next to crying need; immense accumulations of capital alongside pauperism, kept out of sight in the slums of Rome. Inevitably, government corruption came next. Sensuality rather than modesty set the tone in public opinion. The masses, carried away by poverty and passion, stood poised to revolt, murder, and plunder.

Jesus: More Than a Social Reformer

As austere Rome, like sunny Greece, began to sink away into the morass of human misery,[29] a light arose in Bethlehem and a death cry was heard from Golgotha, awakening a new hope for the nations. This was not a new hope in the sense in which men today want to lower the Christ of God to the status of a social reformer. His honorary title, far higher and far richer, was *Savior of the world*. But still, the godliness he wrought among men holds a promise "for the present life and also for the life to come" (1 Tim 4:8)—though Jesus always emphasized that man's eternal welfare comes first, lest soul and body are destroyed in hell [see Matt 10:28]. The worm that never dies, the wailing and the gnashing of teeth in a fire that is never quenched—these were the horrors that gave Jesus no rest as he looked upon the poor human race. The joy to which he called people had to be the eternal joy of his kingdom. The heartlessness of the socialist was never found in the Savior. The socialist, for the sake of improving the lot of humanity in this short span of temporal existence, furiously and recklessly cuts off all prospects of a glory that will endure for all eternity.[30] Neither Jesus nor his apostles ever preached revolution. We are to be subject to every power set over us, and poor Lazarus will be avenged,[31] not while surviving on the crumbs that fall from the rich man's table, but once the rich man suffers eternal torment and poor Lazarus is comforted [see Luke 16:9–31].

If you then ask what Jesus did to bring deliverance from the social needs of his time, here is the answer. He knew that those defiant abuses had sprung from the malignant roots of error and sin, so he confronted the error with truth and broke the power of sin by shedding his blood for that sin and pouring out his Holy Spirit into the hearts of his own. Rich and poor had lost touch as a result of losing their common focus on God, so he called both back to their Father who is in heaven.[32] He realized that the idolatry of money kills nobility in the human heart, so he held up the "service of Mamon"[33] before his followers as an object of profound contempt. He understood the curse that lies in capital, especially for men of great wealth, so he called out to them to stop accumulating capital and laying up treasures on earth where moth and rust corrupt and thieves break in and steal (see Matt 6:19, 20). Jesus turned away the rich young ruler who could not decide to sell *all* that he had and give to the poor (see Matt 19:16–22). The heart of Jesus did not nurse hatred against the rich but a deep compassion for their pitiable state. Serving Mamon is hard, and it is easier for a camel to pass through the eye of a needle than for a rich man to enter into the kingdom of heaven (see Matt 19:24).[34] Jesus got angry only when the possession of money led to usury and harshness. In one of his parables, the man who refused to forgive his debtor is given over to tormentors and branded as a wicked servant who knows no pity.

By Personal Example

Nor did Jesus limit his work to moral motivation. He practiced what he preached. Where poor and rich were at odds he never chose the side of the wealthier but always joined the poorer. He was born in a stable, and while foxes had holes and birds of the air had nests the Son of Man had nowhere to lay his head (see Matt 8:20).[35] His apostles were not allowed to raise funds; they were to go out without purse or provision. True, one of them carried a purse, but that was Judas, that terrible man who was seduced by love of money and sold his soul to the devil.[36] The powerful trait of compassion is inscribed on every page of the Gospel whenever Jesus came into contact with the suffering and the oppressed. He did not reject the people "who do not have the law" [Rom 2:14], but drew them to himself. He would not quench the smoking flax [see Isa 42:3]. He healed the sick. He did not shy away from touching the leper. And when the crowd grew hungry, even though they did not yet hunger after the bread of life, he supplied more than enough loaves of bread and more than plenty of fine fish (see Matt 14:14–21).[37]

In this way Jesus coupled theory with practice. His theory was in tune with the prayer of the writer of Proverbs: "Give me neither poverty nor riches; feed me with the food that is needful for me" (Prov 30:8). It is a prayer from which the apostle draws this lesson for the lover of money:

> For we brought nothing into the world, and we cannot take anything out of the world. But if we have food and clothing, with these we will be content. But those who desire to be rich fall into temptation, into a snare, into many senseless and harmful desires that plunge people into ruin and destruction. For the love of money is a root of all kinds of evils. It is through this craving that some have wandered away from the faith and pierced themselves with many pangs. But as for you, O man of God, flee these things. (1 Tim 6:7–11)[38]

But Jesus' "theory" also implied, inversely, that the poor man ought not to grumble, nor let himself be goaded into bitterness and so vent his worries in anxious questions like, "What shall I eat, or what shall I drink, or with what shall I clothe myself?" "For the Gentiles seek after all these things, and your heavenly Father knows that you need them all." And then follows what is exactly the reverse of what the socialist teaches: "But seek first the kingdom of God and his righteousness, and all these things will be added to you" (Matt 6:25–33).

Organizing the Church

Such is the "theory." It cuts both ways: it cuts the root of sin in the human heart of both rich and poor.[39] But then the theory is also followed up with the heart-conquering practice of devotion, of self-sacrifice—and yet more: of a divine compassion that first pours all the balm at its disposal into the wounds of suffering mankind, and then finishes, for rich and poor alike, by going as a lamb to the slaughter and as a sheep that is mute before her shearers (see Isa 53:7).

Those acts alone, my friends, that message, such a death, would certainly have been enough in and of themselves to exercise an influence for good on social relations. Overthrowing the idol of Mamon and refocusing life's purpose from earth to heaven must by themselves have brought about a complete revolution in people's outlook on life.

But Jesus did not stop there. He also organized. He sent out a church among the nations, an organization that was bound to impact society in three ways. First, through the ministry of the Word, to the extent that the Word constantly combats the lust for money, comforts the poor and the oppressed, and points to a glory without end in exchange for the sufferings of the present time [see Rom 8:18]. Second, through an organized ministry of benevolence that in the name of the Lord, who is the single owner of all goods, demands the community of goods in the sense that it will not be tolerated in the circle of believers that a man or a woman should go hungry or lack clothing. And third, through instituting the equality of brothers so as to offset differences in rank and station. He abolished all artificial divisions between men by joining rich and poor in one holy food at the Lord's Supper, as a symbol of the unity that binds them together not only as "children of men" but also, more importantly, as those who are bowed down under the same guilt and have been saved by one and the same sacrifice in Christ.[40]

It is a fact, therefore, that as a direct result of the coming of Christ and the spread of his church among the nations, society became markedly different from what it had been during the pagan era. Roman society of that time was a striking example of what Jesus once called "whitewashed tombs, which outwardly appear beautiful, but within are full of dead people's bones" [Matt 23:27].[41] The whited sepulcher of Rome crumbled into ruins. And short of claiming that the new social order which in due time arose on those ruins corresponded in any way to the ideal that Jesus cherished, yet we may gratefully acknowledge that it gave birth to more tolerable social conditions. No longer did earthly welfare weigh heaviest in public estimation; eternal well-being also carried weight. Slavery was severed at its root and subjected to a moral criticism that ultimately spelled its demise as an institution. The poor and the orphans began to be cared for. The prohibition of usury helped to discourage the accumulation of too much capital. The higher and lower classes approached each other more freely on a more equal footing. And although the contrast between surplus and scarcity was not eradicated, no longer did excessive luxury clash blatantly with grinding poverty. Society was not yet where it should be, but it was set on a better course. And if the church had not strayed from her simplicity and heavenly ideal, the influence of the Christian religion on political institutions and societal relationships would eventually have become dominant.[42]

For that to happen, however, the pace of evangelizing Europe was too rapid and the diversity of peoples to be assimilated too massive. The conversion of Constantine was a signal for the church to wed herself to worldly power, thereby cutting the nerve of her strength. Hence the gradual infiltration of the church by the world. In the place of disciples who went forth without purse or provision came richly endowed prelates seated in magnificent palaces; and the fisherman from Galilee was succeeded at the head of the Church of Rome by popes surrounded by princely pageantry. A Julius II or a Leo X seemed more intent on paganizing Christendom than on Christianizing the world.[43] The salt had lost its savor and social corruption regained its former strength, a corruption that was checked but not conquered in the countries of the Reformation and that continued to fester in those parts of Europe that remained Roman Catholic. Here, royal absolutism and aristocratic pride in the end evoked the unbearable social tension that at last erupted in a revolution on French—that is, Roman Catholic—soil.[44]

III. The Socialist Challenge

The French Revolution, a revolution that every consistent thinker who professes Christ simply must oppose, did its evil work not so much in that it ousted the Bourbons from the throne, nor in that it made the middle class more powerful than clergy and nobility, but in that it completely overturned people's worldview and outlook on life.

While the Christian religion teaches that the union of Authority and Freedom is guaranteed by the fundamental principle that all men are subject to God, the French Revolution cast out the majesty of the Lord in order to set up an artificial authority based on individual free will, an authority that resembled the kind of scaffolding nailed together of loose planks and beams, which at the first storm-wind will creak and collapse. While the Christian religion teaches man to appreciate life on earth as part of an eternal existence, the French Revolution denied and fought everything that falls outside the horizon of our earthly life. While the Christian religion speaks of a paradise lost, a state of purity from which we fell, and for that reason calls us to humble repentance, the French Revolution saw in the state of nature the standard for what is normal for humans, incited us to pride, and replaced repentance with a liberalizing of man's mind and spirit. Still more, while the Christian religion, as the fruit of divine compassion, introduced the world to a love that wells up from God, the French Revolution opposed this with the egoism of a passionate struggle for possessions. And, to get to the real point that lies at the heart of the social question: while the Christian religion seeks the dignity of the human person in the relationships of an organically integrated society, the French Revolution disrupted that organic tissue, severed those social bonds, and finally, with its atomistic tinkering, left us with nothing but the solitary, self-seeking individual that asserts its independence.[45]

With that, the die was cast. Inevitably, given this wrenching apart of everything that gives human life its dignified coherence, this change gave birth to both deep-seated social distress and a widespread social-democratic movement, as well as an extremely complex social problem that is now facing every nation. I do not deny that other factors contributed to the deterioration of social relationships, such as the application of steam power to machinery, along with faster communication between countries and rapid population growth.[46] But I do stand by my assertion that neither the social question, which now holds two continents in feverish tension, nor the social-democratic movement, which today threatens the public order in Europe and America, could ever have assumed such ominous proportions if the principles of the French Revolution had not brought about so radical a change in the consciousness of nations, classes, and individuals.[47]

Social Distress

In the first place, then, the French Revolution was bound to bring about profound social distress. This followed from its very nature: first, it made the possession of money the highest good, and then it set every man against his fellow man in the pursuit of money. It was not that the Revolution's program mentioned money, or that her more inspired spokesmen did not coax more idealistic tones from their harps. But the theory, the system, could only end in kneeling before Mamon, simply because it cut off the prospect of eternal life and directed men to seek happiness on earth, hence in earthly things. This created a base atmosphere in which everything was valued in terms of money and anything was sacrificed for money. Add to that the demolition of all social organization, followed by the proclamation of the mercantile gospel of *laissez faire, laissez passer* [let do, let pass], and you will understand how the "struggle for life" was ushered in by a struggle for money. The law of the animal world, dog eat dog, became the basic rule for all social interaction. Love of money, chasing after money, so the apostle had taught us, was the root of all evil. Accordingly, no sooner had this evil demon been set loose at the beginning of the nineteenth century, than no plan seemed too subtle, no trick too sly, no deception too shameful to those people who—through superiority of knowledge, position, and capital—took money, always more money, from the socially weaker members of society.

This would have happened even if the opportunities at the start of the struggle had been equal for both parties. But it turned out to be much worse when the opportunities were so manifestly unequal. On the side of the bourgeoisie there was experience and insight, ability and solidarity, ready money and ready influence. On the other side were the peasantry and the working class, destitute of knowledge and deprived of resources, and compelled every morning by the need to feed mouths to accede to any conditions, no matter how unjust.[48] A person did not need to be a prophet to predict the outcome of this struggle. It simply could not end in any other way than in sucking all surplus value toward the capitalists, big or small, to leave the broad lower strata of society with only so much as appeared strictly necessary for keeping them alive as instruments for feeding capital (since in this system labor counted for nothing more). And so a social situation hitherto found only among the Jews—"at one extreme of the social divide the millionaires, at the other end the toilers and drudges, poor as dirt"—gradually became the social situation of all Europe, but now without the palliative of family ties and compassion for poverty-stricken coreligionists that has always had an ameliorating effect among our Jewish fellow citizens.[49] And so the current situation in Europe consists of a well-fed bourgeoisie ruling over an impoverished working class that exists for the purpose of steadily increasing the capital of the ruling class, and is doomed to allow those who are no longer of any use to capital to sink into the morass of the proletariat.

And this social distress is made still worse by the bourgeois practice of instilling false needs in the poor by making a display of its wealth, and of undermining the contentment that can leave men happy with little by igniting in them—all the stronger in the measure that there is less for the poor to enjoy—a feverish passion for pleasure.[50]

Social Democracy

With the same iron necessity the system gave birth, in the second place, to a social-democratic movement, with its open proclamation of a coming revolution. The French Revolution had written on her blood-red banner not only "liberty" but also "equality and fraternity," and the French peasants and the French workers were certainly not the last ones who, singing the Marseillaise, had rushed to the battlefield in the wars of the French Republic to lay hold of these precious ideals. But alas, the equality they dreamed of turned out to be an increasingly offensive inequality, and for the promised fraternity they got a reprise of the fable of the wolf and the lamb.

Was it not natural, then, that the suffering class of society began to ask: "With what right are these drastic conditions imposed on us? They told us we were as good as anybody else and that the numerical minority had to submit to the majority. Well, aren't we the majority, the largest sector of the population by far, the overwhelming masses? And is it not a violation of the basic premise of the Revolution, and a mockery of the sacred rallying cry for which so much blood has flowed in Paris, that a new aristocracy—this time an aristocracy of much lower caliber, an aristocracy of money—stands poised to lay down the law to us, to put its foot on our neck, and so reinstate the evil once overthrown with such incredible exertions by the Voltaires and Rousseaus and the heroes of the Bastille? Give us—yes, us too—the voice in affairs that is owed us according to the system of the Revolution itself. Then we shall outvote you and install a totally different social order that will once for all deliver the deathblow to privilege and finally, finally, give us what your fine theory promised us but that you never gave us."

In all seriousness, Gentlemen, I cannot see how anyone who is not an opponent but a supporter of the French Revolution can have objections, based on sound logical grounds, to this demand from social democrats. From their standpoint at least I must give them my unconditional support. Once the false theory is granted, social democracy, and it alone, is consistent.[51] And as for the common reproach that it is wrong at least in this, that it openly preaches revolution and declares that if need be it will not shrink from using violence, of this too I do not see how one can condemn it in the name of the French Revolution. Or did the dignified gentlemen of the party of the Girondins[52] *not* preach revolution? Did men really sentence Louis XVI to death on the ground that the social order may *not* be breached?[53] Did the spiritual forebears of our liberals and conservatives really shrink from using violence during the September Massacres?[54] But surely to raise these questions is to lapse into absurdity when the dull thud of the guillotine still echoes tragically and troublingly in our ears and when only recently the centennial of the storming of the Bastille[55] was celebrated by all Europe's liberals as the commemoration of a most praiseworthy act of heroism. How can one who has himself not hesitated to wade through streams of blood to achieve his goal, turn other people over to public contempt when they in turn, if caught in a tight corner, would reintroduce the guillotine?

Of course I shudder as I utter these words, and everything with which the Christian religion inspires us recoils with horror from statements such as these. But when comparing the social democrat to the liberal, I cannot fault him. It is using a double standard, it is hypocrisy or self-deception, for those who were born of the Revolution—indeed, born of regicide—to count it as a mortal sin in their own spiritual children when they in turn so much as dare to speak of "drastic measures."[56]

The Social Question

But now I come to a more attractive subject. The French Revolution had a third consequence, this time in the reaction to it. After bringing about the social distress and giving rise to the movement of social democracy, the Revolution also called attention to the social question. Not that the social question is raised for the first time today—rather, it was debated in ancient times, along both the Euphrates and the Tiber, in both Sparta and Athens. It resurfaced when the feudal system made inroads, and again centuries later when it had worn out. And, to add a fact from our own history, it was resolved twice on Java, once when the cultivation system was introduced, and again when it was abolished.[57] In any case, to speak of a social question today means in the most general sense to raise grave doubts about the soundness of the social structure in which we live. The result has been a public debate about firmer foundations on which a more effective social edifice can be erected, this time more livable.[58]

In and of itself, therefore, to raise the question in no way implies that the answer must be found in a socialistic sense. The solution adopted may be quite different. Just one thing is required if the "social question" is to be real for you: namely, that you realize that the current condition of society cannot be continued, and that this condition cannot be explained from incidental causes but from a fault line in the very foundation of our social order. If you fail to realize this and think the evil can be exorcized by fostering greater piety, kindlier treatment and ampler charity, you may think that we face a religious question, or a philanthropic question, but not a *social* question.[59] The social question is not a reality for you until you level an architectonic critique at human society as such and accordingly deem a different arrangement of the social order desirable, and also possible. With regard to the impossibility of continuing the current condition of society, born as it is of the individualism of the French Revolution, I think there can be little difference of opinion among Christians. If a human heart still beats in your breast and the ideal of our holy gospel has ever inspired you, then every higher aspiration you may have must cry out against the current state of society. If this situation continues, life will become less and less a heaven and more and more something of a hell on earth. Our society is drifting away from Christ; it lies prostrate before Mamon. The very foundations of the earth, as the psalmist would lament (see Psa 11:3 and Psa 82:5), are tottering under the steady goad of the most brazen egoism. All the joists and anchors of the social edifice are shifting; disorganization is breeding demoralization; and the drunken revelry of some people in the face of the mounting need of others reminds you more of a decomposing corpse than of the fresh bloom and robust energy of flourishing health.[60]

No, things need not stay this way. We can do better than this. And conditions can unquestionably be made better in the way of—I do not shrink from the word—*socialism*. Only, do not take the word in the sense of social democracy but in the sense, in itself so beautiful, that our country is not (to speak with Da Costa) "a heap of souls on a hunk of soil" but a *community* willed by God, a living human *organism*. It is not a mechanism assembled of component parts, nor a mosaic that forms a "fragmented surface," as Beets[61] calls it, but a body with members, standing under the law of life that we are all members of one another, so that the eye cannot do without the foot or the foot without the eye [see 1 Cor 12:21]. It is this human, this scientific, this Christian truth that the French Revolution ignored, denied, insulted. And it is at bottom the individualism born of this denial that all of today's society is moving away from.[62]

Socialism Is No Temporary Fad

You are mistaken, therefore, if you believe that present-day socialism owes its rise to the confused utopias of fanatics or that it stems from the brains of starving hotheads. Marlo, who in three thick volumes first discussed the "organization of labor,"[63] was a very learned university professor.[64] Rodbertus,[65] who championed the cause of the working classes even prior to Karl Marx, had been a minister of the king of Prussia in 1848.[66] Marx himself, the founder of the First International,[67] belonged to the upper class and married into a ruling family.[68] Lassalle[69] moved in the circles of high society.[70] Henry George[71] was an American from a respectable family.[72] And Schaeffle, in 1871, who went so far as to advocate the collective ownership of land, capital, and the means of production, was a minister of the emperor of Austria.[73] Thus it was almost impossible at times not to burst out laughing when until recently socialism would be talked about, also in our own circles, as something peculiar to the riffraff. One almost wonders whether people read at all, or stay in touch with the times. Did Quack speak to deaf ears when in eloquent prose he introduced the whole family of socialists to our educated public?[74] Indeed, have people never even heard of Plato, the greatest of the Greek philosophers, who drafted and recommended a scheme for a full-scale socialistic arrangement of the state?[75] Such extreme ignorance about the aims of the socialist movement may have been excusable twenty years ago, but today it would lead only to policies that are hopelessly out of date.

In the meantime, the socialist movement has already given birth to four different schools. It has spontaneously and simultaneously given a rude awakening to the "satisfied bourgeoisie" in every country of Europe. It has found its advocates in a whole string of universities and is making the printing presses groan under a constant stream of scholarly studies. It has gradually gained so much in depth and scope and significance that Chancellor Bismarck follows its lead and Pope Leo has circulated an encyclical about it. The German emperor even inaugurated his reign by convening a congress in Prussia's capital for preparing an international solution to the social question.[76]

Truly, it will not do to bury our heads in the sand. There is no strength in scoffing at the slogan "Justice for All," in declaring Domela Nieuwenhuis[77] a social outcast, in letting the ignorant masses jeer, "All the socials in a herring barrel." Socialism is in the air. The social wind, which can at any moment turn into a storm, is swelling the sails of the ship of state. And it may safely be said that the social question has become *the* question, the burning life-question at the close of this century. Indeed, in the whole of this century, so fraught with problems, no problem has emerged that reaches so deeply into the life of the nations and agitates public opinion so vehemently.[78]

The common characteristic of all the forms and stages in which this impressive movement has thus far appeared, is a rising sense of community—of the rights of community and the organic nature of society—in opposition to the one-dimensional individualism with which the French Revolution has impregnated our society, along with its corresponding economic school of *laissez faire, laissez passer.* This zeal for the social principle is so strong that it has led to a battle over property rights and a war on capitalism, given that the individual finds his strongest bulwark precisely in his property. Absolute property rights have allowed immense fortunes to be amassed, which now form an insurmountable obstacle preventing society from doing justice to its sociological nature.[79]

The Unity and Diversity of Socialism

Thus the socialist movement in all its branches stands united in opposing individualism. But no sooner is the question raised about what should be demolished and what should be erected in its place, than *tot capita tot sensus*—there are as many opinions as there are heads. After all, people who do not believe in God to whose eternal ordinances we are to submit, and who do not attach much importance in the life of nations to historical development that never permits its intrinsic law of life to be violated with impunity—such people look upon the entire structure of contemporary society as nothing but a product of human convention. Hence they consider themselves perfectly justified in razing it to the ground. Nor do they shrink from the gigantic task of building anew on the vacant plot.

Of those who think along these lines, the most radical is the nihilist. He realizes that everything hangs together in life and he therefore believes society cannot be saved so long as every last remnant of our deadlocked civilization still stands. Hence he wants to start by destroying everything, literally everything. His ideal is to return to the time immediately after the flood. He does not halt until he has reached *nihil*—nothing.[80]

A degree less radical is the anarchist. He laughs at this idea that the very houses and tools are infected and instead locates the virus only in government and in every force and function that emanates from government. For the anarchist, the demolition will have gone far enough once government is abolished. No more state; only a society. Then the golden age will arrive in due course.[81]

Still less radical are the social democrats. They would keep both state and society, but a state that is merely the organ and house manager of society. The state should be so arranged that the *many* households are dissolved into the *single* household of the state and that in this one household all citizens share equally. True, there are nuances among them: relentless fanatics who preach rioting and looting, alongside men like Liebknecht[82] who hope to triumph through parliamentary action; a Schaeffle who advocates common ownership of land, capital, and the means of production, next to the ordinary collectivist who would have the state own only the land and the means. But at the end of the day their paths all converge in one and the same ideal: a state that absorbs all individuals into itself and looks after all individuals equally.[83]

At a fair distance from these social democrats you find the state socialists. They reverse the above position, albeit with a variation, by placing the authority of the state high above society, but then also charging state authority with the task of guiding the movement of society in a top-down manner.[84] This school has found its enthusiastic spokesmen in Rudolf Meyer, Adolf Wagner, and partly in Emile de Laveleye, along with many others; and it has finally found its ideal statesman in Bismarck.[85]

As for the Historical School, its strength lies less in a practical program than in scholarly research. It hopes to be able to dispel the illusion that current conditions and legal relationships are of a timeless nature. It thus prepares public opinion for change, and it investigates what would make for orderly change.[86]

Add to this list the less doctrinaire liberals. One can detect among them a growing inclination, on the one hand, to become more conservative—that is, to make the necessary concessions for preserving the status quo—and, on the other hand, to become more radical by enlarging the political influence of the lower class in order to improve its lot and to curtail the self-destructive privileges of the propertied class.[87]

To complete this brief summary, finally, I add the cynical pessimists. These men acknowledge that something is smoldering in the house of our modern civilization. They will even concede that there is a fire and that if the fire is not checked the flame of an all-destructive revolution will soon break out. Yet they declare at the same time that extinguishing the fire will simply prove impossible. Thus they prophesy with stoic calm that our modern civilization, like the ancient Near Eastern and Greco-Roman civilizations, is destined to sink into Nirvana.[88]

IV. A Christian Approach to the Problem of Poverty

If I am not mistaken, Gentlemen, with this hasty sketch I have achieved my goal of highlighting the threads by which the Christian religion must be woven together with the problem of poverty. What remains for me to do in this final part of my address, therefore, is to take up these threads one by one and show you what direction they ought to give to our study of the problem and to our response to it.

But first I must clear up one final question which, if left unanswered, would probably nullify the force of my argument. The question is this: How can I call social democracy a fruit of the French Revolution and at the same time contend that it is opposed to the basic principle of the French Revolution? This apparent contradiction stems from the fact that the individualistic character of the French Revolution is only a derived principle. It is not its root principle from which it drew its dynamic. That root principle is its defiant cry *Ni Dieu, ni maître!* [No God, no master!] Or, if you will: humanity's emancipation from God and from the order instituted by him. This principle gives rise to two lines, not just one. The first line is the one that leads you to dismantle the existing order and leave nothing standing except the individual with his own free will and his supposed supremacy. But alongside this line runs another, at the end of which you are tempted not only to push God and his order aside, but also to go on and, deifying yourself, sit in the seat of God (as the prophet said [see Ezek 28:2]); and from your own head you create a new order of things. That's what social democracy is doing. Yet even as it is busy doing so, it gives up very little of the individualistic starting point. Underneath the social structure that it seeks to erect—allow me to use an image from the building trade in Amsterdam—it still drives the piles of popular sovereignty, and hence of individual wills, through the medium of universal suffrage.[89]

Response to Socialism

But this only in passing. The question that now demands our full attention is this: What attitude should Christians adopt in the face of the socialist movement?

And then it is beyond question that we too should be moved to profound compassion by the disorder of our society and the great distress that has resulted from it. We may not, like the priest and the Levite, pass by the exhausted traveler who lies bleeding from his wounds, but like the good Samaritan we ought to be moved by a holy compassion for him. Yes indeed, people are suffering; there are crying needs.[90] Those needs may not yet be so great in the circles of our regular tradespeople, but they certainly exist among the proletariat behind them, and no less in certain rural areas. Think of Friesland.[91] And then I join Bilderdijk and say: God has not willed that a person should toil away and still not have enough to feed himself and his family, let alone that someone with able hands and a will to work might, just because there is no work, die of starvation or be condemned to begging.[92]

To be sure, if we have "food and clothing" the apostle would have us be content with these (see 1 Tim 6:8 or Prov 27:26).[93] But there is no excuse for a situation in which our heavenly Father with divine generosity causes an abundance of food to come forth from the ground and that through our fault this bounty is distributed so unequally that while one person has more than enough to eat the other goes to bed with an empty stomach—if he even has a bed. And if there are people who want to defend such abuses by invoking—God forgive them—the words of Jesus, "For the poor you always have with you" [John 12:8], then out of respect for God's holy Word I must register a protest against such a misuse of Scripture. I must ask those who so judge first to study the same Scripture, so that they can see how conditions for the poor in Israel were almost luxurious compared to the wretchedness in which our proletariat are sunk.[94]

If you then ask me whether charitable giving should increase even more, then I answer without a moment's hesitation, *most certainly!* But I hasten to add that a charity that knows only how to give money and not how to give one's self, is not yet Christian love. You will not be blameless unless you also give of your time, energy, sympathy, and resourcefulness to help end such abuses once and for all. You will remain blameworthy until you leave nothing unused that lies hidden in the storehouse of your Christian religion for combating the cancer that is destroying the vitality of our society in such alarming ways. The material need is appalling and the oppression is great. And you fail to honor God's Word if you should ever forget that Christ himself, just as his apostles after him and the prophets before him, invariably took the side of the suffering and the oppressed against the rich and the mighty of this world.

But even greater, and more appalling, is the spiritual need of our generation. When in the midst of our social misery I observe the demoralization that follows on the heels of material need, and hear a raucous voice that, instead of calling on the Father in heaven for deliverance, curses God, mocks his Word, insults the cross of Golgotha, and silences whatever voice still testifies in his conscience—all in order to set aflame, as in a rage, everything untamed and brutish in the human heart—then, my friends,

I stare into an abyss of spiritual misery that moves me to pity almost more than the most grinding poverty.

This spiritual misery, too, cries out in reproach of us as Christians. Were not almost all those who now rage once baptized? And following their baptism, what has been spent on those thousands to make them understand something—at least something— of the true love of God that there is in Christ Jesus, instead of the caricature of the Christian religion against which they now utter their curses? And when the poison of the French Revolution crept undetected into the veins of the social body, what have we Christians done in our country to stop the poisoning of the lifeblood of society? Indeed, when at last the evil erupted and the social disease assumed epidemic proportions, what has been our contribution toward offering medicine and balm for its cure? Only now are we making our first feeble attempt by means of a social congress to face up to society's deadly struggle. By this time, our Christian intellectuals should already have been laboring for twenty or thirty years with something of the earnestness and scholarly approach of a Marlo or a Schaeffle to plumb the depths of this desperate situation.[95]

Spiritual and Social Problems

There is so much damage to make up for! Just consider the issues involved. Of primary importance is the majesty of our God. Although I shall presently discuss some concrete measures, we must first take up those general ideas that give shape and color to our entire outlook on life. We are neither plant nor animal; being human is our badge of honor; and because we are human we live first of all as conscious beings, and our sense of happiness or unhappiness in many ways is governed by our notions, ideas, and general concepts. Therefore the first article of any social program that is to bring healing must remain: "I believe in God the Father Almighty, Maker of heaven and earth." This article is today being erased. Men will no longer hear of God in politics. Not because they do not find the poetry of religion charming, but because to say "I believe in God" is to acknowledge that there is a divine order for nature and a divine ordinance for our conscience—a higher will, to which we creatures have to submit.

Today, everything has to be a free product of human creativity. The social edifice has to be erected according to man's whim and caprice. That is why God has to go, so that men, no longer restrained by natural bonds, can invert every moral precept into its opposite and subvert every pillar of human society. Does that not point us in the direction we ought to go precisely when dealing with the social question? As Christians we are to emphasize as strongly as possible the majesty of God's authority and the absolute validity of his ordinances. For all our condemnation of the rotting structure of our society, we are never to help erect any structure other than one that rests on the foundation laid by God.[96]

Just as surely, in the second place, we Christians are to take sides in the controversy between state and society. If you, like the social democrats, allow the state to be absorbed by society, you deny the political authority that God has established to uphold his supremacy and his justice. Conversely, if you, in line with the state socialists, allow society to be absorbed by the state, you offer incense to the deification of the state. You will be putting the state in the place of God and destroying a divinely ordered, free society for the sake of the apotheosis of the state. Against both positions we Christians must uphold the view that state and society each has its own sphere, or, if you will, each has its own sovereignty, and that the social question cannot be properly resolved unless we respect this duality and thus honor political authority while also clearing the way for initiatives from society.[97]

If, in the third place, the question is raised whether our human society is an aggregate of individuals or an organic body, then all those who are Christians must place themselves on the side of the social movement and against liberalism, simply because God's Word teaches us that we are made of one blood and joined in one covenant [see Acts 17:26–31]. And we must do this no less because both the solidarity of our guilt and the mystery of the atonement on Golgotha are absolutely incompatible with all such individualism and point instead to the cohesive whole that is human society.[98]

If then the pantheist, and inspired by him the pessimist, call out to us that the process of history, however fatal and miserable, cannot be disturbed—that an iron fate governs the course of human life and that we must first wade through this river of woe in order to arrive perhaps in later years at happier circumstances—then it is our duty as Christians, with God's Word in hand, to resist this false theory of blind fate as well as the false system of culpable passivity. On the basis of our confession of God's providence we are to separate, also in society, what is good from what is evil. With a sword at our side and a trowel in our hand, we must simultaneously contend against what has been found untenable and reinforce what has proved beneficial.

Or if, in the fifth place, the hot-headed zealot, in direct opposition to this passive pessimism, tries to set fire to the house and through wild revolution hopes to clear the ground for erecting the new building, then it is just as much our duty as Christians, with the apostolic Word on our lips, to warn against all violation of authority, to oppose boldly every act of violence or lawlessness, and to insist loudly that the line of historical development must never be carried forward except through gradual transition and along lawful avenues.[99]

In the sixth place, if the social question places the issue of property on the agenda, and the one claims that property rights are absolute while another wants all private property to be converted to communal property, then the person who lives by God's Word must oppose this with the only true theory that God gave us in his ordinances. In God's name he has to bear witness that there can be no question of absolute ownership except in the case of God himself, and that all our possessions are only held on loan from him. We manage our possessions only as a form of stewardship. This means on the one hand that none but God the Lord can release us from our responsibility for managing those possessions; but on the other hand that we can never have any other property right than in association with the organic coherence of mankind, hence also with the organic coherence of mankind's goods. Thus what the social democrats call "community of goods" existed neither in ancient Israel nor in the first Christian community.[100] On the contrary, an absolute community of this kind is everywhere precluded in Scripture. However, Scripture does preclude just as surely any presumption of a property right on the strength of which you could dispose of your property absolutely, as though you were a god over it, without taking the needs of others into consideration.[101]

Furthermore, if both collectivists and also advocates of the nationalization of land have made a separate issue of the question of the land, then it is appropriate for us as Christians neither to arrogantly ridicule such a notion, nor to shrug our shoulders at such a thorny issue as though God's Word gives us no guidance here. Our conscience alone won't let us. We hear how in Scotland three-fourths of all the land is in the hands of fourteen persons, and how not so long ago one of those fourteen who had purchased a new tract, inhabited by forty-eight families, simply evicted the almost three hundred persons living there in order to extend his game preserve. If we hear this, surely an inner voice tells us that a "right" like this to dispose of land from which bread for the consumer must grow just cannot be right, as a matter of principle; and treating ownership of land the same as ownership of goods must run counter to God's ordinances. Israel's laws laid down quite distinct rules for land ownership. The fertile field is given by God to all the people, so that all the tribes of Israel might dwell on it and live off it. Any regulation of land ownership that does not reckon with this explicit ordinance ruins land and people.[102]

O, it is so profoundly untrue that the Word of God only calls us to save our souls. No, God's Word poses firm ordinances and draws unmistakable lines also for our life as a nation and for our common social life; and we Christians are unfaithful to God's Word if we disregard this fact and conveniently allow our theory and our practice to be determined by the opinion of the day or by prevailing laws.[103]

The Power and Clarity of God's Word

At almost every point in regard to the social question, God's Word provides the most specific directives. Think of the family, whose immediate destruction is being advocated; of marriage, which some men would transpose into free love; of family ties between the generations, which some propose to dissolve by repealing laws of succession; and no less of births, which they wish to regulate by law. Did not Bilderdijk—to start with the last issue—even before he knew of Malthus, denounce, on the basis of God's Word, all such agitation as an *impium facinus*, a godless deed, contrary to God's positive ordinances; a *homicidium posteritatis*, a murder of unborn offspring?[104]

For precisely the same reason we may never, so long as God's Word has authority among us, be opposed to colonization. God's earth, once cultivated, can produce food aplenty for more than double the millions who inhabit it today. And what else is it but human folly to crowd together in a few spots on the globe so that people have to hide in cellars and slums, while whole regions elsewhere, a hundred times the size of our entire country, await the plough and the sickle, or where thousands of herds of the most magnificent cattle roam without an owner. "Be fruitful," says the divine commandment; but also: "fill the earth" (Gen 1:28); and not: "crowd together on a little plot within your narrow borders."[105] For indeed, marriage, which suffers harm as a result of such crammed geography, must be held in high honor by Christians, and God punishes us with all the calumny of the sin of sensuality and the curse of prostitution when we resist his ordinance in this matter.[106]

Thus the same Word of God prefigures and prescribes the family household as that wondrous creation from which the rich fabric of man's organic life is to develop. Here too you need not hesitate; you know what you have to do. We do not have to organize society; we have only to develop the germ of organization that God himself implanted in our human nature. Away, therefore, with false individualism, and anathema on every effort to break up the family! In the civil society on Dutch soil, at any rate, where for three centuries family life has flourished as a source of resilience, the dismantling of this primary foundation of our society must never be allowed—at least not with our consent.[107]

The issue is no different when it comes to labor. Specifically with regard to physical work, which speaks most loudly in the social question, what stands out is the divine ordinance: "By the sweat of your face you shall eat bread" (Gen 3:19).[108] But standing next to it is also this word: "The laborer deserves his wages" (Luke 10:7). And you shall not defraud him of his wage (see Jas 5:4), much less withhold it from him (see Deut 25:4). The Lord says expressly through Moses: "You shall not oppress a hired worker who is poor and needy" (Deut 24:14); his wages may not even be kept with you overnight (see Lev 19:13). You shall honor the workingman as a human being, of one blood with you; to degrade him to a mere tool is to treat your own flesh as a stranger (see Mal 2:10). The worker, too, must be able to live as a person created in the image of God. He must be able to fulfill his calling as husband and father. He too has a soul to care for, and therefore he must be able to serve his God just as well as you. That is why he has a right to a Sabbath—a right that is especially important for one whose work tends to pull him down to a material level. The worker, too, was created by God as a frail creature, as one whose strength breaks under sickness and accident and also diminishes with age. And even then, when he can no longer toil in the sweat of his brow, he should be able to eat bread from the labor of the days of his manly strength.

So speaks God in his Word, and your workman reads that too. He must read it, and he should read it. And when he reads it, does not God's Word itself give him the right—no, not to grumble, even less to revolt, but at least to *complain*? May he not lodge a complaint against a social order that deprives him so painfully of that which an ordinance of divine mercy had intended for him? And although this suffering is felt by few of us personally, should it not weigh upon us for our brothers' sake? With God's Word in hand, may we hold back from leveling a withering critique on so diseased a society? Indeed, quite apart from the question of public relief, may we be at ease so long as that society is not reformed in accordance with God's Word? To treat the working-man simply as a "factor of production" is to violate his human dignity. Worse, it is a sin that goes squarely against the sixth commandment, "You shall not kill"—which also covers killing the workingman socioeconomically.[109]

A brief word, finally, about public relief. God the Lord unmistakably laid down the basic rule also for the calling of government. Government exists to administer his justice on earth and to uphold that justice. Thus its duty is not to take over the tasks of family and society; the state should withdraw its hands from them. But as soon as collisions arise from contacts between the different spheres of life so that one sphere encroaches upon or violates the divinely ordained domain of another, then a government has the God-given duty to uphold rights against arbitrary acts and to push back the stronger party in the name of God's rights to both spheres. What a government may not do under any circumstances is to grant legal protection to one sphere and withhold it from another. A Commercial Code—I stand by what I said in parliament back in 1876[110]—also calls for a Labor Code. Governments should give workers their rights. Labor, too, should have the opportunity to organize itself and stand up for its rights.

And as for the other type of state aid, which consists of distributing money, not justice, under whatever form and pretext: that sort of aid, to be sure, was not precluded from Israel's laws either, yet there it was kept to a minimum. Therefore I say, unless you wish to weaken the working classes and break their natural resilience, always limit any material assistance by the state to the smallest dimensions. An enduring solution for nation and country, hence also for our working classes, is found only in powerful private initiative.[111]

So then, no more arguments are needed, Gentlemen, to show that the outlook on human life afforded by the Christian religion provides—for virtually all aspects of the social question—a fixed starting point from which to attempt a concrete solution to each problem. We do not stumble around in the dark. The principles against which we are under obligation to test present-day conditions and current legal relations are clearly expressed in the Word of God. We fall short in our sacred calling as Christian citizens if we shirk the solemn task of reconstructing whatever appears in conflict with God's will and ordinances.

A Balanced Perspective

And yet, I may not end with this. For even if we pursued the path of justice to the end and succeeded in having measures passed that improved the legal situation, we would still never attain the goal God has in view. Legislation by itself will not cure our sick society unless at the same time drops of the medicine enter the hearts of rich and poor. Sin is such a terrible power that it makes a mockery of your dikes and dams. Regardless of your legal system, time and again sin will inundate the terrain of human life with the waters of desire and self-interest.

So I come back to the point I started from a moment ago: because we are conscious beings, almost everything depends on the standard of value that our consciousness brings to bear on life. If this present life is all there is, then I can understand why people want to enjoy it before they die and why they are haunted by the mystery of suffering. And therefore it is your standing duty, you who profess our Lord Jesus Christ, to place life eternal in the foreground for both rich and poor, and to do so earnestly, so that it grabs hold of people, and emphatically, so that it pierces their soul. Only those who reckon with a life everlasting know the true value of this earthly life. If outward possessions, material goods, and sensual pleasures are all that is intended for man, then I can understand the materialist and do not see what right I have to reprove the glutton and the hedonist. Therefore it is your duty, children of the kingdom, to seize every occasion and use every means to impress upon rich and poor that the peace of God is a much greater treasure and that the spiritual well-being of man is of much greater worth.

In the face of poverty, too, it is an open question just how you arrive at contentment and happiness. That depends by no means solely on the sum of your possessions. It depends first of all on the needs that are aroused within you, and on the kind of needs you want to have met. The socialist may sneer that this dismisses the poor with "pie in the sky," but the facts say otherwise.

If you are familiar with our Christian families, including families with the lowest incomes, then you know how much the fear of God can do for those who have only a sober portion of worldly goods. You will have observed how that little portion is elsewhere squandered in alcohol addiction and sin but is twice blessed in the case of the Christian workingman; you can testify how even in a poor household human dignity comes into its own in husband, wife, and children; and you will have thanked God for the generous share of happiness and bliss that they enjoy despite their limited resources.

No, the core of our working people do not ask, and they do not beg. On the contrary, they sometimes give generously to those who have less than they do.[112] I feel strongly that anyone who sets himself up as a prophet among our people and causes these fundamental elements of their consciousness to waver is guilty of cruel and pitiless conduct. Equally cruel for the same reason is the modern theology that is preached from the pulpits, sowing the seeds of doubt in people's hearts about our eternal destiny. No less cruel was our public school, which dragged the children down from this lofty standpoint. What the Christian school has done through this alone for the suffering of our people, when it restored to thousands upon thousands of families this only reliable standard of value for our life, our goods, and our joys, cannot be estimated highly enough.

But this means, Gentlemen, that among those of us who are better off, the whole of our life should be preaching the same holy principles. You who were given more may not willfully fly in the face of those principles by going back to your immoderate attachment to earthly possessions—giving the impression that for you the enjoyment of luxury means more to you than anything else, or even worse, that you share only grudgingly what you have received from the Lord as your Owner. Then the less fortunate do not believe what you preach. And they would be right; for all our sense of truth revolts against a theory about happiness in the hereafter that only serves the purpose of keeping poor Lazarus at arm's length here on earth.

There cannot be two different faiths—one for you and another for the poor. The really decisive question in all this is simply whether you recognize in the less fortunate, indeed in the poorest of the poor, not just a *persona miserabilis*, a wretched creature, but someone of your own flesh and blood and, for Christ's sake, your *brother*. It is exactly this noble sentiment, sad to say, that has been weakened and blunted so brazenly by the materialism of our age. Yes, you know them too, those wealthy owners who are alarmed by the socialist threat and now, from fear of this threat, reach for all kinds of social improvements that none of them ever thought of before. But at least among us who profess the Lord, let a more perfect love—I plead with you—cast out all such fear. There is no room in our ranks for those who wish to march with us in order to safeguard their money box. This is holy ground, and he who would tread on it must first rid the soles of his feet of his egoism. The only voice permitted here is the stirring and eloquent appeal of the good Samaritan whispering in our ears. People are suffering all around you, and these people are your brothers, your natural kin, your own flesh and blood. You might have been in their place and they in your more pleasant position.

The gospel speaks to you of a Savior of humankind who, though he was rich, still for your sakes became poor that he might make you rich [see 2 Cor 8:9]. The gospel makes you kneel in adoration before a Child born unto us, but born in a stable, wrapped in swaddling clothes and laid in a manger. It points you to the Son of God, yet one who became the Son of Man and crossed the land from affluent Judea to poor, despised Galilee to turn to those who were in need or pressed down by sorrow. Indeed, it tells you about this one and only Savior who before he departed from this earth stooped before his disciples in the garb of a slave, washed their feet one by one, and then got back on his feet and said: "I have given you an example, that you also should do just as I have done to you" (John 13:15).[113]

Time for Action

The beauty of a love that comes from God and wells up within you does not display its glory when you allow poor Lazarus to quiet his hunger with the crumbs that fall from your richly laden table [see Luke 16:20–21]. All such charity rather insults a manly heart that beats no less in the poor man's breast. Rather, this love shines forth when, just as rich and poor sit down together at the table of the Lord's Supper, so you feel for the poor man as for a member of the body and you feel for your hired servants and maids as for children of men, human beings like yourself. A well-meant handshake is sometimes sweeter for a poor man than a generous gift of alms. A kind word, spoken without condescension, is the sweetest balm for those grieving with loss. Divine compassion, sympathy, suffering *with* us and *for* us—that was the mystery of Golgotha. So you too, in solidarity with your suffering brothers, must share in their pain. Only then will the sacred music of solace begin to resonate in your words, and then, driven by sympathy and compassion, you will spontaneously make your actions fit your words.

Indeed, *actions*, acts of love, are also crucial. Obviously, the poor man cannot wait until the restoration of our social structure has been completed. Almost certainly he will not live long enough to see that happy day. Nevertheless, he still has to live; he must feed his hungry mouth and the mouths of his hungry family. Robust aid is therefore called for. And however much I am inclined to commend you for your sacrificial giving—and this is true, by the grace of God, of many of you—yet the holy art of "giving for Jesus' sake" [see 2 Cor 4:11] should become much more developed among us Christians. All poverty relief by the state, never forget, always leaves a blot on the honor of your Savior.[114]

Show compassion, therefore, to the depressed and the oppressed. Nothing is more suited than this compassion to make you "imitators of God, as beloved children" [Eph 5:1]. The sacred motive of mercy contains the secret of the heavenly power that you as Christians can exercise. For that wondrous motive makes the miser generous and opens the lips of those who are dour by nature. And when you are then moved to empower the poor through counsel, leadership, and initiative to row against the current of suffering in society, then you will not be at a loss for helpers, but then all real (not just nominal) Christians will vie for the great honor of assisting in this ministry of mercy to your suffering brothers in Jesus' name.

Men and brothers, may this high and holy motive govern our meeting together at this congress. Let none of us boast of the good work that we are about to undertake, but let there be instead a quiet self-reproach that we are meeting only now. And may the happy fact that the men of Patrimonium[115] are meeting and consulting with fellow Christians from the upper class be for us a token of peace, and may it be an inviting prophesy that mutual trust will soon be fully restored among us.[116]

And if you ask me, finally, whether I dare to place any hope in this congress—the hope that we shall at least come a little closer to solving this burning question of the day—then do not forget that the social problem is a global problem, a problem of an eminently international character, one which on that account can never be definitively settled within the narrow boundaries of our small country. What the future will reveal also with respect to this question depends on a host of factors that are not within our power. It could be that our long-provoked God, in his righteous judgment, will allow some very troubling days to come upon us, if not immediately, then in the not-too-distant future. These are the secret things that also at this congress we leave to the Lord our God (see Deut 29:29).[117] But while we await whatever may come, we do have his revealed commandment: to do, also at this congress, whatever our hands find to do, and to do it with all our might [see Eccl 9:10]. May God the Lord grant his blessing to that end.

And furthermore, what is beyond dispute for all of us is this: if our violently disturbed society is yet to be rescued, then our fast-dying century will have to recognize Christ as its Savior. I therefore close with a prayer that I know lives in everybody's heart. It is this: should this rescue be delayed and the stream of iniquity rise still higher, may it never be said of us Christians that because our faith, whether it be among the higher or the lower classes, was so lukewarm, we kept our society from being rescued and we forfeited the blessing of the God of our fathers.[118]

I thank you.

Notes

1. To be sure, one may counter that the more socialist school in economic theory did receive university appointments, in our country as well as abroad. However, it should be noted (1) that when there was talk some years back of appointing a more radical economist to a chair in political economy, the appointment was thwarted and ultimately stopped by [the Ministry in] The Hague; (2) that in other countries appointments went almost exclusively to *state* socialists; and (3) that the Ministry, if need be, is not afraid (as became apparent recently at the state University of Groningen) to appoint a more radical economist, but only because a fundamental unity was assured between the professor and his more orthodox colleagues: both refuse to reckon with special revelation. However, as soon as it is a question of filling a chair in a law faculty with someone who is not only a Christian and a jurist but who wants to be a *Christian jurist*, they will have none of him, either for constitutional law or political economy. Thorbecke, who was very radical for his time, was appointed; Groen van Prinsterer was not.

2. *Ed. note*: Alfred von Waldersee (1832–1904) was a field marshal under Kaiser Wilhelm II. Prominent Christian socialists included the court preacher Adolf Stöcker (1835–1909) and Rev. Rudolf Todt (1839–87), who helped found the Central Union for Social Reform and the Christian Social Workers' Party.

3. *Ed. note*: F. D. Maurice (1805–72) and Charles Kingsley (1819–75) were Anglican clergymen and founders of "Christian Socialism" in Britain. Stewart Headlam (1847–1924) was an Anglican priest whose activism was explicitly inspired by Maurice and Kingsley.

4. This association was founded in Geneva in the spring of 1888, on the initiative of Mr. Frédéric Necker. I call attention to the following articles in its bylaws:

> ART. 1
>
> The goal of the Christian Society of Social Economics is to gain insight into prevailing social conditions in Switzerland that are contrary to the laws of justice, charity, and solidarity which according to the very order of God must govern relations among men, and to bring about their reform by the use of means that are in harmony with these laws.

ART. 2

Placing itself outside all political, ecclesiastical, or theological interests, it appeals to all those who acknowledge Jesus Christ as their Master and who believe that applying the principles taught in his gospel is the solution to all the questions affecting the happiness of every individual in particular and the progress of humanity in general.

ART. 3

It accepts as members all persons who, adhering to these views and principles, wish to cooperate in whatever way toward their realization.

ART. 4

It proposes to attain its goal by stimulating, through conferences or otherwise, the study of all relevant topics, by issuing publications from time to time, by taking up contact with associations that pursue a similar goal, and finally by affirming through all possible means the duty incumbent upon Christians to work toward the moral and material well-being of the masses.

ART. 5

The foregoing provisions may not be changed by the General Assembly unless the proposed changes have been approved by three quarters of the members of the Association.

In the opening address by Mr. Necker on Feb. 18, 1889, the goal of the Society is explained further in these words:

It is therefore not enough to help the unfortunate privately, or even to combat this or that cause of the suffering. We must find out whether we cannot take collective measures more generally and get at the misery in all its sources at once. We must acquire special knowledge, for these complicated problems are not solved with instinct or enthusiasm. That is what our discussion must be about. At the same time, all members [of the steering committee] agree that, in order to acknowledge that Christ has come to bring to mankind salvation and healing of all their ills, the true remedy can only be found in the application of his teachings.

Thus our conclusion is that it was not only useful but necessary to establish an association that can guide Christians in gaining better than usual insight into the current conditions of the social order that cannot fail to make enemies of order and especially enemies of the gospel, and to seek a solution to problems which interest all men to such a high degree.

See *Bulletin No. 1* (Geneva, 1889), 9–10. Last year the Society published *Quatre écoles d'économie sociale, conférences données à l'Aula de l'université de Genève* [Four socio-economic schools: Lectures delivered in the auditorium of the University of Geneva] (Paris: Fischbacher, 1890), a publication we recommend highly. The Roman Catholic position of Frédéric Le Play is explained by Claudio Jannet, socialistic collectivism by G. Stiegler, state socialism by Charles Gide, and the liberal or classical school by Frédéric Passy. A similar Christian association exists in France under the name Protestant Association for Practical Study of Social Questions [*Association protestante française pour l'Etude pratique des questions sociales*]. Its *Bulletin* is included in the *Revue de Théologie pratique et d'études sociales*.

5. We must admit, to our shame, that the Roman Catholics are far ahead of us in their study of the social question—very far in fact. Although the school of Le Play—who in his well-known works *La Réforme sociale en France*, 2 vols. (Paris: E. Dentu, 1866); *L'Organisation du travail* (Tours: A. Mame, 1870); and *L'Organisation de la famille* (Paris: Téqui, 1871), more or less went his own way—is not identical with the Catholic school, still we do not ignore that men like Ketteler, Christoph Moufang, Claudio Jannet, Albert de Mun, Charles-Emile Freppel, Charles Périn and others have not only engaged in serious study of the social question but have also laid out the direction we should follow. *La question agraire* (Paris: Retaux-Bray, 1887), by Rudolf Meyer and G. Ardent; *Le Patron: sa fonction, ses devoirs, ses responsbilités*, and *De la richesse dans les sociétés chrétiennes* (Paris: Victor Lecoffre, 1861), by Périn; and to a certain extent also [a work by novelist] Arvède Barine, *L'Oeuvre de Jésus-ouvrier* (Paris: Fischbacher, 1879), provide many surprising insights into the practical ideas of these authors. But Catholic activity is even more impressive when we look at their frequent conferences, their periodical literature, and the associations they have founded. In particular the *Unions de Patrons en faveur des Ouvriers* [Employers' unions for the benefit of workers] in Belgium, about which Rev. Pierson will give more details at our congress, is an excellent undertaking that deserves to be emulated. The clear pronouncements of Cardinal Newman are familiar enough, and although German and French Catholics are somewhat divided—the former lean more toward relying on the State, the latter more toward the Church alone—the encyclical of Leo XIII will probably soon bring them together. Thus Catholic activities should spur us on to show greater energy (although

Catholics *here at home* are still mostly inactive)—all the more so since we Protestants can learn more from the Roman Catholics than from the Knights of Labor in America, who did start out under Stephens in 1869 by requiring an oath on the Bible but abandoned it already in 1878 at the order's assembly in Philadelphia. At the assembly in Richmond in 1886 the entire order went over to socialism lock, stock, and barrel. The *Christlichsoziale Arbeiterspartei*, too, gave us less by comparison, both because it leans too much in the direction of state socialism and because it fails to penetrate to the fundamental principles involved. Precisely the latter was done by the encyclical, and what is more, it dealt solely with those principles that all Christians hold in common and that we too share with our Roman Catholic fellow countrymen.

For the Knights of Labor, see the informative work by Arthur Hadley, *Socialism in the United States* [*Ed. note*: Although Arthur T. Hadley commented widely on economic matters, including the Knights of Labor, efforts to locate a work by this title have been unsuccessful. Kuyper may have intended to refer here to the work of another prominent economist of that era, Richard T. Ely, such as *Recent American Socialism* (Baltimore: Johns Hopkins University Press, 1885), and "Socialism in America," *North American Review* 142, no. 355 (June 1886): 519–25], and Amédée Villard, *Le Socialisme moderne; son dernier état* (Paris: Guillaumin, 1889), 190. A good survey of the Catholic movement is Landelin Winterer, *Le socialisme international; Coup d'oeil sur le mouvement socialiste de 1885 à 1890* (Paris: Lecoffre; Mühlhausen: Gangloff, 1890).

6. *Ed. note*: Frédéric Le Play (1802–82), French engineer turned sociologist who launched the systematic study of the family in industrial society.

7. *Ed. note*: Wilhelm von Ketteler (1811–77), bishop of Mainz, pioneer of Christian social thought in Germany.

8. *Ed. note*: Leo XIII, encyclical letter *Rerum Novarum* (May 15, 1891).

9. *Ed. note*: Willem Bilderdijk (1756–1831) and Isaac da Costa (1798–1860) were Dutch poets associated with the *Réveil* ("revival"), an evangelical reform movement in the Netherlands with similarities and connections to evangelical revivals elsewhere in Europe, including England and Switzerland. Guillaume (Willem) Groen van Prinsterer (1801–76) was the leading member of the "confes-

sional" party in the Dutch Reformed Church and founding father
of the antirevolutionary movement in Dutch politics.

10. W. Bilderdijk, *Nieuwe Oprakeling* (Dordrecht: J. de Vos 1827), 43,
46, 47. R. A. Kollewijn, *Bilderdijk, zijn leven en werken*, 2 vols.
(Amsterdam: Van Holkema and Warendorf, 1891), 2:136, also
points to this trait in Bilderdijk's reflections. To some extent one
may even look upon Bilderdijk as a forerunner of state socialism
insofar as he demanded that the state provide every twenty-year-
old young man the chance to be in a position to marry. See his
Briefwisseling met Tydeman, 2 vols. (Sneek: Van Druten & Bleeker,
1866–67), 2:67ff.

11. *Da Costa's kompleete dichtwerken*, 3 vols. (Haarlem: A. C. Kruseman,
1861–63), 2:397; see also, besides his *Bezwaren tegen den geest
der eeuw* [Grievances against the spirit of the age] (Leiden: L.
Herdingh, 1823), his magnificent song "De Vrijheid" [Freedom], p.
364; and no less his depiction of socialist misery in London, woven
into his "Wachter, wat is er van de nacht?" [Watchman, what of
the night?], 3:87; as well as his occasional poem "1648–1848,"
3:113ff., esp. 119.

12. *Ed. note*: G. Groen van Prinsterer, *Adviezen in de Tweede Kamer
der Staten-Generaal*, 2 vols. (Utrecht: Kemink en Zoon, 1856–57),
2:556–573, at 571; speech of Dec. 19, 1853.

13. G. Groen van Prinsterer, *Nederlandsche Gedachten*, 2nd ser.,
6 vols. (Amsterdam: H. Höveker, 1869–76), 4:64. In a speech in
the lower house of parliament on June 18, 1850, Groen warned:
"It is the misfortune of our age that men set democracy apart.
It will do us no good to give power to the middle classes. They
too are a new aristocracy and a new privileged class, and it will
only mean a transition." G. Groen van Prinsterer, *Adviezen in
de Tweede Kamer der Staten-Generaal, zitting van 1849–1850*,
2 vols. (Amsterdam: Johannes Müller, 1851), 2:125. That for the
rest Groen expected improvement only from a better organization of society is clear from the following: "Our worst ailment is
pauperism. Poverty, unemployment; ruptured relations between
the higher and lower classes; no bond save work and pay; prole-
tarians and capitalists. Where this will take us is uncertain; but
there is no doubt where it came from. From *liberty and equality* as
understood by the Revolution. Just one detail. When that slogan
was first raised, guilds and corporations too had to go. The desire
was for free competition; no restraints on skills and industry; no
hateful monopolies exercised by individuals or associations; the

development of private initiative and commerce would guarantee a better future. Well, the future that was envisioned has arrived. Can it be called better? *On this point I am of one voice with the leading spokesmen of the present-day revolution.* It is this liberty, this unrestricted competition, this removal, as much as possible, of the natural relationship between employer and employee, which tears the social bonds, ends in the dominance of the rich and the rule of the banking houses, robs artisans of regular sustenance, splits society up into two hostile camps, gives rise to a countless host of paupers, prepares for the attack by the have-nots on the well-to-do and would in many people's eyes render such a deed excusable, if not legitimate. It has brought Europe to a state so dreary and somber as to cause many to call out in terror: Is there no way to revive, in some altered form, the associations that were so recklessly crushed under the revolutionary ruins?" G. Groen van Prinsterer, *Vrijheid, Gelijkheid, Broederschap; toelichting op de spreuk der Revolutie* (The Hague: L. Van Nifterik, 1848), 83–84.

14. See *Freiland und die Freilandbewegung* (Dresden: E. Pierson, 1891), 57. The quotation occurs in Theodor Hertzka, *Freiland. ein soziales Zukunftsbild* (Dresden: E. Pierson, 1890), 275. This constant appeal by socialists to Christ should be neither underestimated nor overrated. Two motives are at work here. First, it is a tool of propaganda, since they know how easy it is to gain a hearing the moment one appeals to Scripture. But it is also a misguided belief. Some socialists are indeed struck by the glaring contrast between the way Christ viewed the social need and the long-standing attitude toward this need adopted by many Christians. In both cases there is an implicit acknowledgment of the authority that Scripture still exercises, and that is a joyful sign. A utopia similar to *Freiland* has been written, besides Bellamy in his *Looking Backward 2000–1887* (Boston: Ticknor and Company, 1888), by the American Ismar Thiusen (pseud.) in his *Looking Forward; or The Diothas* (London: G. P. Putnam's Sons, 1890).

15. A. Naquet, *Socialisme collectiviste et socialisme libéral* (Paris: E. Dentu, 1890), vi.

16. These beautiful words are quoted in the foreword to *Quatre écoles d'économie sociale*, vi.

17. *Ed. note*: Although advertisements for the congress had explicitly invited women to attend, Kuyper throughout addressed his audience as *Mijne Heeren* ("Milords" or "Gentlemen").

18. A mistake that is often made is that people associate the Christian religion solely with the world of feeling. To be sure, even in this respect its significance for the social question is great, insofar as a great deal depends on the state of feeling in rich and poor, in government officials and citizens, and even in the public interpreters and commentators. He who can contribute even a little to improve these feelings does an excellent work. But the Christian religion is mutilated when its action is confined to the world of emotions. It professes not just Christ but the Triune God—Father, Son, and Holy Spirit—for which reason its first article of faith is: "I believe in God the Father Almighty, Maker of heaven and earth." This implies that the Christian religion must also have a position on our relation to nature, government, and our fellow man, including human nature and its attributes—a position on the very phenomena that govern the social problem.

19. I concede that the word *art* is commonly used only for those arts that call for aesthetic appreciation. Yet the word itself does not limit it to that, and usage, even today, allows a broader denotation. At bottom, *art* simply denotes a power given to man to wrestle free from the overpowering force of nature. Only because man's triumph over nature comes out best when he manages to portray the idea of nature more beautifully than nature itself, is free, creative art today called art in a more restricted sense.

20. See Gen 2:15, where it says literally: "The LORD God took the man and put him in the garden of Eden to work it and keep it." The notion of "keeping" can only mean that man was charged with barring all influence of Satan. After all, there was no other enemy, and Satan could enter Eden only through man's heart. And as for the word "work" (*'abad*), this cannot refer to plowing and digging, which is contrary to the whole character of Paradise, but must be taken in the sense of that higher cultivation that human art works upon nature.

21. Belgic Confession, art. 12.

22. *Ed. note*: A formula associated with the *Réveil*.

23. Human societies too are partly a work of nature, partly a product of human art. For things to go well, human art in the political and social domains should not violate nature or cripple its power, but guide and develop it. Further, it may not regulate this guidance of nature and of the nations in an arbitrary fashion, but must do so according to the ordinances of God that are given both in his

Word and in the idea of man. The mistake of the French Revolution was that in its arrogance it rejected historical statecraft; in part it wanted to regress to undeveloped nature, and in part wished to remake the existing state of affairs according to its own insights. Similarly, the theory of nationalities embraced by Napoleon III was a one-sided emphasis on the nature of peoples at the price of human art in this area. That said, both were understandable reactions to the sinful approach of our former diplomats, politicians, and jurists, who considered nations an abstraction, a kind of *corpus vile* [worthless body] that could be experimented with at one's pleasure.

24. The two powers of error and sin must always be sharply distinguished if one wishes to understand the development of social life. A third power is also operative, that of necessity independent of human involvement; this power can be left out of consideration here, although it is a fact that this necessity too, which is mostly the consequence of wars, insurrections, and disasters, is just as much related to sin. But in this connection we must note two other powers that give direction to social life, namely the power of custom and the power of the law. The power of custom is the collective expression of a nation's predispositions and arises imperceptibly; but customs are also given a certain direction in every domain by the great and mighty of this world, and no less by the intellectuals and philosophers who by influencing the nation's ideas gradually alter the nation's predispositions as well. But besides these two influences the condition of society depends on a country's laws, especially in those states and those times in which the law is less governed by the national spirit than the national spirit by the law. Exactly for this reason every mistake committed in this area must always be accounted for in terms of sin. Sin, on the one hand by the darkening of our mind (in error) and on the other by the weakening of our will (in direct sin), turns the impact of our human art upon society into a curse instead of a blessing. This might not be noticed right away, and popular leaders and statesmen only seldom realize sufficiently their awesome responsibility in this regard. Nevertheless, in this way too God visits a righteous judgment on the peoples—peoples that are themselves the reason why human art in the social domain in part falls short and in part corrupts so much, and why art then ends up seeking to restore its strength in the frenzy of revolution. See Louis-Mathurin Moreau-Christophe, *Du problème de la misère et de sa solution, chez les peuples anciens et modernes*, 3 vols. (Paris: Guillaumin, 1851).

25. Only from this point of view does one understand the French Revolution at one and the same time as horribly necessary and deeply sinful. State policies had gradually led the nations down impassable paths and had done such violence to human nature that a reaction became inexorable. Things had to bend or break. The statecraft of the time should have repented of its unnatural ways and of its own accord infused fresh air into the oppressive atmosphere. Failing that, the political fabric could only be torn to shreds. Nature always reacts when art tries to force it. To that extent a violent explosion was bound to come, and the French Revolution was indeed a righteous judgment of God on those who had misused the power and fortune entrusted to them. Yet this in no way diminishes the deeply sinful character of the French Revolution insofar as it separated, contrary to God's ordinances, nature from history and replaced the will of the Creator of nations with the will of the individual. This stamped it as a movement opposed in principle to God and his Christ, and for that very reason, after a short breathing spell, it brought a corruption deadlier than the corruption it revolted against in 1789.

26. The Crown, it is said, must stand above the parties and act against the superior power of the majority in the interest of the minority whenever needed. That is correct, yet it is only a derived thesis. At the basis of it lies the more general thesis that government is the minister of God and thus must defend the oppressed in God's name, since God takes pity on the oppressed. This is how it must be in the courts when justice is dispensed. This is how it must be with the police when violence erupts. And similarly in the life of society, government through its laws and regulations must take care to preserve the balance and protect the weaker members. To view civil government as the organ and instrument of the majority of the moment is therefore a deeply sinful conception of the task of the magistracy. Then government lines up with those who are already the stronger, in order to oppress the weaker even more; this leads to reaction and anarchy, and ultimately fosters nihilism.

27. Many Bible readers, and also many preachers, make the mistake of reading or discussing moving words like these without applying them directly to the reality of their own environment.

28. If words as strong as these were not found in the Bible and someone were to venture today to write them down at his own initiative, he would be branded a crypto-socialist. For those who want to pin their hope on money and the power of money, Scripture is a

hopeless book. The Holy Spirit who speaks in Scripture happens to consider an abundance of gold and silver more dangerous than desirable, and he deems an inheritance of millions not comparable by far to the inheritance that awaits us among the saints. This is what God attests in his Word, so I may not represent it any other way. And let no one reproach me for it, but let him realize that his criticism would attack Scripture itself.

29. One cannot pay enough attention to the parallel between the social conditions that preceded the fall of the Roman Empire and the social evils in the midst of which we ourselves are living today. Naturally, the forms were different then; but the imbalance was the same; and if the popular press had existed at that time and newspapers had been handed down to us, journalists would almost be able to copy whole articles from them. The moral props of that society were moldy and rotten, as they are today. Roman civilization, excelling in cultural refinements, finally collapsed. Similarly, our Western civilization will eventually succumb, unless the Christian religion, which is still a vital force, intervenes to save it. But in and of itself the danger is no less now than it was then.

And if someone says that it was the barbarian invasions that delivered the deathblow to the Roman Empire, then we ask whether the growing power of Russia, and partly of the Chinese that hide behind Russia, has nothing to say to us today. See Moreau-Christophe, *Du problème de la misère*.

30. This heartlessness can only be accounted for by the fact that the scholars and the educated began by first undermining the belief in a life after this life, and then eradicated it. Doubt is no first step to faith, and to speak of a "hope of immortality" is tantamount to destroying belief in an eternal existence, at least with the masses. I therefore stand by my use of the term "heartless." Socialists may not personally believe in an eternal life, but neither can they prove the contrary. Is it then not heartless—equate eternal life, for the sake of concreteness, with a thousand years—to entice someone to pursue happiness for say, seventy years, and then have him pay for this with a wretched existence of upwards of nine centuries? And what are a thousand years when measured against eternity?

31. I do not shrink from using the word "avenged." Scripture forbids us to abandon this idea. "You will only observe with your eyes and see the *punishment* of the wicked," says Psalm 91:8 [NIV]. This idea is not at all out of step with what Jesus teaches us in the

Gospel: in his parable about Lazarus he lets him *see* the anxious suffering of the rich man, and he even has the rich man appeal to Lazarus's pity to deliver him from his pain.

32. That this really is implied in the name of Father is evident from Malachi 2:10, where the prophet asks in the name of the Lord: "Have we not all one Father? Has not one God created us? Why then are we faithless to one another, profaning the covenant of our fathers?" The Lord's Prayer, too, clearly expresses the same thought. In that prayer the poor prays for the rich, that God may give him his bread for that day, and the rich prays the same for the poor. Nowhere does this prayer talk of *me* or *I*, but always of *we* and *us*: "*Our* Father in heaven, forgive *us our* debts. Give *us* this day *our* daily bread" [Matt 6:9,12,11].

33. *Mamon* (not *Mammon*) is a word in Aramaic that means *capital*. It is personified by Jesus in Matt 6:24, to place it directly opposite Jehovah. Mamon is often spoken of in the same breath with the "golden calf," but wrongly so. The worship of the golden calf in the desert did not stem from greed; the Israelites had all sacrificed their gold to make that golden calf; besides, what they worshiped in this calf was not gold but Jehovah, under the symbol of a power of nature. No, the Scriptural term that serves as the stigma of the worship of capital is the worship of Mamon. The sinful nature of this worship consists in this, that the rich possess wealth not as belonging to the Lord but as though it belonged to them—which then exacts its price in that they fancy they are master of their money whereas money becomes their master. See Otto Wittelshöfer, *Untersuchungen über das Kapital, seine Natur und Function* (Tübingen: Laupp, 1890), who may not be writing from our perspective yet who clearly shows the power inherent in capital. See also Johann Karl Rodbertus, *Das Kapital. Vierter sozialen Brief an Von Kirchmann*, ed. Theophil Kozak (Berlin: Putttkammer & Mühlbrecht, 1884), and Franz Stöpel, *Das Geld in der gegenwärtige Wirtschaft* (Minden: Bruns, 1885).

34. Too little notice is taken of this trenchant statement of Jesus and too few sermons deal with this text. This saying does not rebuke the rich but shows compassion and pity for them. The struggle to repent is so much more difficult for them than for the poor. In light of one's eternal well-being it is an advantage to be poor. Well-considered, a rich man who becomes a true child of God is a double manifestation of God's liberating grace. There is just one thing the Lord does not tolerate: when a rich man dares to oppress a poor

man! Then the Lord's wrath is kindled, as is so clearly shown in the parable of the unforgiving servant (see Matt 18:23–35).

35. Jesus had no possessions and no earnings. He lived on gifts of love. I prefer to emphasize this rather than the fact that Jesus had been a workingman. In this I follow Scripture, which tells us nowhere that as a youth Jesus did carpentry work. Not that I would deny this; I even consider it probable; but it is not part of the Gospels' message. However, the Gospels do oblige us to point out that Jesus belonged to the have-nots and lived off gifts of money and goods.

36. Judas carried the money bag (John 12:6; 13:29). To be the treasurer is always dangerous. Dealing with money makes a man materialistic. Money as such has a bad influence on a man's heart. That is why it is so unhealthy for a nation when banking and the stock exchange become dominant. And that is also why it is precisely the man of high finance for whom the chance to learn to bow humbly before his God is so remote. Bilderdijk realized this when he wrote Da Costa: "It requires no explanation that merchants and professional gamblers have no Christian faith." See Kollewijn, *Bilderdijk, zijn leven en werken*, 2:137.

37. When reading stories like these we tend to put the emphasis too exclusively on the miracle. Yet the Gospel writer introduces the story by saying: "When he went ashore he saw a great crowd, and he had compassion on them." Jesus helped out with bread and supplemented it with fish; his distribution to the poor was not scanty but generous. Those who have to do the hardest work should be fed the heartiest food.

38. The word that our authorized version [the *Statenvertaling* of 1637] uses for the root of all evil is *geldgierigheid* [miserliness]; but that is not how to read it today. To be a miser today is to commit the sin of stinginess. A miser hoards his money and does not want to spend any of it. But in the seventeenth century *geldgierigheid* meant exactly what it says in the original Greek: *philargyria*, that is, hungering, lusting, after money. Today we call this *geldzucht* [avarice]. There are today, alas, money-grubbers among those who call themselves Christians who live a lavish lifestyle and then think: "I am certainly not tightfisted, so this root of all evil does not apply to me."

39. Jesus flattered no one, neither rich nor poor, but put both in their place. That is why Jesus has such high standing. Prominent men in our society generally look down upon the poor and flatter the

rich, or else they scoff at the rich while flattering the poor. This is contrary to the Christian religion. Both must be convicted of their sin. Still, it is true that when Scripture corrects the poor it does so much more tenderly and gently; and, by contrast, when it rebukes the rich it uses much harsher language. However, our poor too will gradually lose the faith if they pin their hopes on all kinds of help from the state instead of relying solely on their Father who is in heaven.

40. Far too little attention has been paid thus far to the fact that Jesus not only preached but also organized. His circle of three disciples, then twelve, and then seventy, already spoke of an organization; but not until the installation of apostles and deacons and the commission to proclaim the Word and administer the sacraments was that gigantic organization called into existence that has gradually spread to all nations throughout the centuries. And now it is worth noting how this organization was instituted not only for securing the eternal welfare of its followers but most definitely also for removing social ills. This organization produced these twin fruits precisely on account of its divine simplicity. This fact alone tells us that the Church abandons its principle when she concerns herself only with heaven and fails to relieve earthly need, and that our diaconates will have to function very differently if they would truly honor Christ.

41. On this, see Charles Letourneau, *L'evolution de la propriété* (Paris: Vigot Frères, 1889), 332ff., and Louis Morosti, *Les problèmes du paupérisme; la vérité sur la propriété et le travail*, 2nd ed. (Paris: A. Ghio, 1887).

42. On this, see the work of Wilhelm Endemann, *Die national-ökonomischen Grundsätze der canonistische Lehre* (Jena: Friedrich Mauke, 1863), vol. 1 in B. Hildebrand, ed., *Jahrbücher für Nationalökonomie und Statistik*. Indeed, the rise of a "system of economic theories and economic policies, developed with phenomenal consistency," was due to "the basic principles of the Christian religion." See Wilhelm Roscher, *Geschichte der National-Oekonomik in Deutschland*, 2 vols. (Munich: R. Oldenbourg, 1874), 1:11.

43. In this connection we should certainly not forget that the voluntary poverty of the monastics was an attempt to carry on the original tradition, and to that extent the vow of poverty was a well-intentioned protest against growing worldliness in the church. But, aside from the question whether such vows are lawful, it is a matter

of historical record that the monasteries of that age turned the vow of poverty more and more into a fiction. And even if they had remained more faithful to their ideal, the monastics could never have made amends for the immeasurable damage that the church herself inflicted on social relationships by her pursuit of worldly splendor. As long as she was persecuted the church flourished and ennobled social relations. When she came into a position of honor under Constantine it was at the price of her moral influence. As a result she had no choice but to throw her weight on that side of the balance of power that was exactly opposite to where Jesus had put it.

44. On the considerable influence that the Protestant Reformation had on the improvement of social conditions, read Roscher, *Geschichte der National-Oekonomik in Deutschland*, 1:82–120. It is worthy of note that Roscher dates the weakening of this influence from the rise of territorialism, a system of political economy that had its roots in the Lutheran Reformation, not the Calvinian. He does not hesitate, therefore, in acknowledging that our country in particular gave the first impulse toward more correct economic insights. "It is beyond dispute that economic primacy in Europe passed from Upper and Central Italy to Holland" (p. 223). Compare Étienne Laspeyres, *Geschichte der Niederländischen National-Oeconomie* (Leipzig: S. Hirzel, 1863).

What I say about Catholic countries in no way speaks of anti-papism, but facts are facts, and as long as Catholics persist in painting Calvinism as the root of the Revolution we are obliged to point to the notorious fact that the great Revolution broke out in a Catholic country, that still today Southern Europe and South America are entirely Roman Catholic and at the same time the most revolutionary, and that the Throne is nowhere safer than in Protestant countries.

45. This is the pivot on which the whole social question turns. The French Revolution, and in the same way, present-day liberalism, is anti-social; and the social distress that today disturbs Europe is the evil fruit of the individualism that was enthroned with the French Revolution. In France especially this has never been understood by most Christians, including Protestants. As is well known, the school of Vinet chose individualism, of all things, as its basic premise. Guizot alone saw deeper and therefore better—at least in his second period. This explains why most French Christians, led by De Pressensé, became fellow travelers with the revolutionaries

and why their example was followed in other countries as well, our country not excluded. [*Ed. note*: François Guizot (1787–1874) was a right-wing liberal in the French government, but after the 1848 revolution he renounced his liberal past. Edmond de Pressensé (1824–91) was a student of the theologian Alexandre Vinet (1797–1847) and served as a pastor of the Evangelical Church in Paris. He was appointed senator for life after holding a seat in the French National Assembly where he was a staunch advocate of the separation of church and state.]

46. It is just as one-sided to try and explain the social ills almost exclusively in terms of steam power and machine production as it is to shut one's eyes to these factors. Usually, however, the effect of the machine is overemphasized. If morality and personal faith had not been so defiantly undermined by the French Revolution, the class struggle would never have assumed such formidable proportions. Machines and steam simply present us with an inner contradiction: steam power improved the lot of the worker and relieved drudgery, but the endless division of labor dulls the mind, lowers the value of manual labor, and when one machine can do the work of a hundred it puts ninety-nine men out on the street.

47. This change is most apparent nowadays in the entirely different outlook on life found in the great cities and the rural areas. It explains why the lower rural classes, even though their condition is often more wretched than that of the lower urban classes, actually live happier lives and complain far less than their counterparts in the city. One can also discern this in Patrimonium [*Ed. note*: A Reformed workers' association founded in 1876]. How vastly different its tone from that heard in socialistic groups!

48. This fact simply cannot be denied. Inevitably, capital absorbs more and more capital until it meets a resistance it cannot break. That resistance, in the present context, is the fact that workers cannot possibly make ends meet at present wage levels. Whatever else one may say, Lassalle is perfectly correct in saying that this iron law of wages is the curse of our society. And yet this law is the natural consequence of *laissez faire, laissez passer*—or if you will, of unrestricted competition. Capital absorbs more capital in this way not because of any evil purpose, but simply because it does not meet with any other power of resistance short of "to be or not to be" of the workers—of the instruments that feed capital. See Ernest Gilon, *Maatschappelijke nooden*, trans. G. Keller Jr. (Amsterdam: H. Gerlings, 1889). The complete system of *laissez*

faire, laissez passer is given in Adam Smith's *The Wealth of Nations*, 3 vols. (London: Cadell and Davies, 1812 [1776]). This work is edited and annotated, among others, by J. F. Baart, *Adam Smith en zijn onderzoek naar den rijkdom der volken* (Leiden: Van Der Hoek, 1858). In the meantime, John Stuart Mill in his *Principles of Political Economy*, 2 vols. (London: John W. Parker, 1848) has put a lot of water in this economic wine. See also Thedor Hertzka, *Die Gesetzen der sozialen Entwicklung* (Leipzig: Duncker & Humblot, 1886).

49. I am prepared to acknowledge the sincere efforts liberalism has made to advance the lower class. But what did it offer them? Reading, writing, and arithmetic! And what did it take away from them? Faith, the courage to live, and moral energy. What did it withhold from them? Trade schools and a share in capital.

50. In this respect, the displays in our shop windows do more evil than people realize. In many ways they stimulate covetousness and create needs that, if not eventually satisfied, leave behind a feeling of bitter discontent. Similarly, the excessive luxury of our school buildings has done harm to a class of pupils who at home can never live in such a grand style. Happiness is not an absolute but a relative concept. He who awakens needs that he is in no position to satisfy shoulders a big responsibility and commits an act of callous cruelty.

51. It is not enough to say that the social-democratic movement issues from the liberal theory. It must also be stressed that the liberal calls for a totally arbitrary halt on a trajectory that according to his theory has to be followed. Thus the liberal has spiritual kinship with the social democrat, but unlike him he is in the wrong, because he is arbitrary, self-serving, and inconsistent.

52. *Ed. note*: The Girondins were early participants in the Revolution who preached moderation yet voted in favor of deposing the king.

53. *Ed. note*: The main charge for which King Louis XVI was condemned to death was that he had "conspired against liberty."

54. *Ed. note*: In the September Massacres during the Revolution, crowds in Paris dragged imprisoned "traitors to the sovereign people" from their cells and murdered them.

55. *Ed. note*: Early event in the Revolution, when a prison fortress was captured by a Paris mob that set the prisoners free and lynched the garrison.

56. It is indeed passing strange how many of the ordinary citizens in our country at one and the same time condemn the advocacy of force on the part of the social democrats and yet praise the French Revolution to the skies. Surely it won't do to say that the September Massacres were merely *excesses*. After all, without *revolution* there would have been no Revolution in 1789. Every liberal, even if one does not hold the excesses against him personally, nevertheless bears responsibility for the revolutionary use of force. What it comes down to is that force is considered legitimate when used to the advantage of the liberals but is abhorred the moment it tends to undermine their power. Hence in 1845, also in our country—in [the liberal daily] the *Arnhemsche Courant* at that—there were allusions to regicide, and today the appearance in parliament of a social democrat offends "respectable" liberals. See Eugen Jäger, *Die Französische Revolution und die Soziale Bewegung* (Berlin: Puttkammer, 1890).

57. *Ed. note*: Kuyper discusses the rise and demise of the colonial government's system of compulsory cultivation in his work *Our Program: A Christian Political Manifesto*, trans. and ed. Harry Van Dyke (Bellingham, WA: Lexham Press, 2015), §§251–56.

58. These essential characteristics of the social question must be carefully kept in mind. That is not to say that the social structure has to be taken down wholesale and replaced with a brand new one. History always asserts its rights, and there can never be a question of total demolition. Even when men fancy they are busy doing so, they aren't really; history's influence is too powerful. But neither can you say that the job is done after you have applied a few dabs of paint and replaced a roof tile here and there. No, you must definitely cordon off the house and put up scaffolding. The structure won't do any longer. The repair that is required is far too comprehensive for that. See Anon., *Personal and Social Evolution with the Key of the Science of History* (London: Fisher Unwin, 1890); Hertzka, *Die Gesetzen der sozialen Entwicklung*.

59. I am not saying that the religious and philanthropic aspects of the problem are unimportant, but merely that one who looks no further and extends his antennae no further than this has not yet come in touch with the social question.

60. Applying blush to your skin does not make it less dull but only worsens your unhealthy complexion. So it is with our society. It lives with more cultural refinements; it clothes itself more styl-

ishly (though not more beautifully); it pretends to be glowing with youth. But he who is no stranger to the dressing rooms of high society, and sometimes sees the matron in her negligee, knows all too well how faded and jaded she actually looks.

61. *Ed. note*: Nicolaas Beets (1814–1903) was a theologian of the ethical-irenical school and author of a collection of poems, *Brokkelvloer van rijmspreuken* (The Hague: M. M. Couvée, 1891).

62. The beautiful word "social" should not be left to the private preserve of social democrats. Christianity is preeminently social. The beautiful picture that the apostle Paul paints for us of the social nature of the church in 1 Corinthians 12:12–27 and no less in Ephesians 4:16 is *mutatis mutandis* equally applicable to human society. In fact, we believe that, rightly viewed, the original organism of humanity, now purified, has been resurrected in the church of Christ. See F. D. Maurice, *Social Morality: Twenty-one Lectures Delivered in the University of Cambridge* (London: Macmillan, 1890).

63. Karl Marlo, *Untersuchungen über die Organisation der Arbeit, oder System der Weltöconomie*, 3 vols. (Kassel: Wilhelm Appel, 1853).

64. *Ed. note*: Karl Marlo, pseudonym for Karl Georg Winkelblech (1810–65), taught chemistry in Kassel, Germany, and spent the last twenty years of his life writing in favor of common ownership of the means of production.

65. *Ed. note*: Johann Karl Rodbertus (1805–75) was a gentleman-economist from Pomerania, a province of Prussia along the Baltic Sea. He was a pre-Marxian socialist who wrote widely on land rents, overproduction, economic crises, the labor theory of value, and similar topics.

66. Rodbertus was for a short period minister of worship in the Auerswald–Hansemann cabinet; see Georg Adler, *Rodbertus, der Begründer des wissenschaftlichen Sozialismus* (Leipzig: Duncker & Humblot, 1884). His first work was *Zur Erkenntnis unsrer staatswirthschaftlichen Zustände* (Neubrandenburg: Barnewitz, 1842). His most extensive publication is *Zur Erklärung und Abhülfe der heutigen Creditnoth des Grundbesitzes*, 2 vols. (Jena: Mauke, 1876).

67. *Ed. note*: Karl Marx (1818–83) was the chief theoretician of the communist movement and in 1864 helped organize the First International Workingmen's Association.

68. Like Marlo and Rodbertus, Marx was a man of outstanding erudition and scientific talent. His critique of the Hegelian philosophy of law was masterful and his work *Das Kapital. Kritik der politischen Oeconomie* (Hamburg: Meissner, 1871) was first of all a scholarly study. For those who find this work too demanding, Gabriel Deville wrote *Le Capital de Karl Marx, résumé et accompagné d'un aperçu sur le socialisme scientifique* (Paris: H. Oriol, 1883).

69. *Ed. note*: Ferdinand Lassalle (1825–64), after studying philosophy in Breslau and Berlin, became a lawyer and a social activist who founded the first political party for German workingmen advocating universal male suffrage.

70. Lassalle indeed circulated among the higher classes. In 1864 he was killed in a duel with a Moravian prince who was his rival in seeking the hand of the daughter of an ambassador. His forte was oratorical talent more than scholarship, yet he more than anyone caused the socialist ideas to become widespread in Belgium.

71. Henry George, the apostle of land nationalization, is best known for his book *Progress and Poverty*, which he wrote in 1877–79 especially in connection with the situation of the Jews. The dedication in this fascinating book is touching: "To those who seeing the vice and the misery, feel the possibility of a higher social state, and would strive for its attainment." More than 300,000 copies have already been sold. In the edition of Kegan Paul of London, this work of 400 pages fine print costs only *f*0.60.

72. *Ed. note*: Henry George (1839–97) was a newspaper editor and political economist who played a major role in the rising labor movement in America. His widely popular book *Progress and Poverty* taught that the chief cause of poverty was "unearned wealth" from land rents, and that the solution lay in taxing the value of land.

73. Dr. Albert Eberhard Friedrich Schaeffle was minister of trade in the Hohenwart cabinet. His main work is *Das gesellschaftliche System der menschlichen Wirthschaft*, which in a short time went through three editions. It was published in two volumes by Laupp in Tübingen. [*Ed. note*: Albert Schaeffle (1831–1903) was a profes-

sor of political economy in Tübingen and later in Vienna. In his translated work *The Quintessence of Socialism* (London: Swan Sonnenschein, 1889) he argued for collective ownership and a planned economy.]

74. H. P. G. Quack, *De Socialisten: personen en stelsels*, 3 vols. (Amsterdam: P. N. Van Kampen & Zoon 1875–92). [*Ed. note*: Hendrick Peter Godfried Quack (1834–1917), a liberal who was sympathetic to the plight of the working classes began as a professor of political economy at the University of Utrecht, a post he exchanged after ten years for a senior position at the Bank of the Netherlands, eventually becoming its director.].

75. For those who do not understand any Greek, three of his dialogues, *The Statesman, The Republic*, and *The Laws*, are accessible in excellent translations by [Friedrich] Schleiermacher. A brief but reliable overview of Plato's political system is found in Zeller, *Die Philosophie der Griechen*, 3 vols. (Leipzig: Fues, 1875), 2:756ff. As is well known, Plato carried his socialist and even communist ideas to such lengths that he even abolished the family and wished to declare child-rearing a task of the state.

76. This was a happy move by the Kaiser, even though the result fell far below expectations. Actually he committed plagiarism, because the proposal he took up had already been discussed by Switzerland.

Regardless, little progress will be made this way. The social question can indeed only be solved internationally; but before the several nation-states realize this and venture to act with the energy required, more particularism will have to be overcome than can perhaps be realized short of a general combustion throughout Europe. Instead we are moving in a direction where each nation again thinks only of itself with regard to social problems, and with regard to economic competition each nation is beginning to live at war with all the others, at most seeking security in narrow trade blocs. No one has (unintentionally) brought out this international element more clearly than J. H. von Thünen in his *Der isolirte Staat in Beziehung auf Landwirthschaft und Nationalöconomie*, 3 vols. (Rostock: G. B. Leopold, 1842).

77. *Ed. note*: Ferdinand Domela Nieuwenhuis (1846–1919) was a Lutheran pastor who turned socialist and later anarchist. He supported the Dutch labor movement but ultimately chose for a revolutionary solution to the social question.

78. Nothing is more foolish than to view socialism as a passing storm and a cloud that will evaporate. It is certainly true that the socialists are internally divided and still lack leaders unselfish and high-minded enough to call into being a global action. Their congresses are mostly scenes of tumult, and their publications abound in barbed civilities. But you are mistaken if you view the social question as a temporary inconvenience. On the contrary, the very fact that the socialists, despite their many differences, have made gigantic steps forward shows the dynamic force that social democracy propagates. Don't forget that the International was founded only in 1864, that shortly thereafter it fell apart, that the new association still has a very deficient structure, and yet that the social movement after only a quarter century has thrown all Europe into turmoil. Particularly since the 1889 congresses in Paris its activity has made disturbing advances. Villard, *Le Socialisme moderne*, like the above-mentioned writing of Abbé Winterer, *Le socialisme international*, paints a convincing picture both of the enormous dimensions of this movement and of the significance of the centennial celebration of the French Revolution for its revisionism. See also August Sartorius von Waltershausen, *Der Moderne Sozialismus in den Vereinigten Staaten von Amerika* (Berlin: H. Bahr, 1900) [ET: *The Workers' Movement in The United States, 1879–1885*, ed. David Montgomery and Marcel van der Linden, trans. Harry Drost (New York: Cambridge University Press, 1998)].

79. Of course we are not denying that greed and envy play a big role in the social question. As persons, the members of the class that now complains are no better than the men of the class that has "arrived." People who were poor and became rich usually turn away from socialism; and on the other hand there are no more dangerous socialists than people who have lost their fortune. But evil passion does not call into existence a lasting world movement. The power of socialism does not stem from its covetous desire, but rather from the moral demand of societal life. This demand speaks to men's conscience; here throbs its lifeblood; on this demand religion places its seal. The attack on private property only entered the picture long after this inescapable righteous demand. See Gaëtan Combes de Lestrade, *Eléments de sociologie* (Paris: F. Alcan, 1889); Friedrich Elbogen, *Die Erlösung: sociale studien* (Zurich: Schröter & Meyer, 1889); and Charles Secrétan, *Etudes sociales* (Paris: F. Alcan, 1889).

80. To understand a nihilist, read the portrait of one painted in *Germinal* by Zola, who now has also become a Christian socialist. Actually, the *perhovtri* in Russia go even further by forbidding all marriage in order to make our hopelessly corrupted human race die out; see *Allgemeine Evangelisch-Lutherische Kirchenzeitung*, no. 40, Oct. 2, 1891. A historical survey of nihilism is found in Nicolai Karlowitsch, *Die Entwicklung des Nihilismus*, 3rd ed. (Berlin: Behr, 1880). It did not arise until 1875 and first drew attention as a result of the assassination attempt on General Trepow. Today its strength is broken, but the idea of nihilism is not gone. That idea will return as soon as social democracy pursues its aim with any consistency and wakes up to the influence of the historical past on current conditions. See also Alphons Thun, *Die Geschichte der revolutionären Bewegungen in Russland* (Leipzig: Duncker & Humblot, 1883).

81. The anarchists owe their significance to the Russian writer Bakunin, and as for their organization and the development of their ideas even more to General Kropotkin and Johann Most. Their central committee is stationed in London and its publication was *Die Freiheit*. They were most active in France, Switzerland, Belgium, and North America, where the famous Chicago trial [following the Haymarket affair of 1886] broke their back. Their slogan was "Propaganda of the deed." And at a congress held in London in July, 1881, the rule was adopted that "to achieve the goal we pursue, i.e., the annihilation of sovereigns, ministers, clergy, nobility, big capitalists, and other exploiters, all means are legitimate."

   The Paris Commune of 1871 differed from anarchism in that it wanted to destroy central governments but keep the *commune*, that is, the organization of the local community.

82. *Ed. note*: Wilhelm Liebknecht (1826–1900) was the cofounder of the Socialist Labor Party of Germany, which abandoned revolutionary activity in favor of forming the opposition in parliament and meanwhile educating the working class.

83. The French *possibilists* in particular, as well as the German social democrats under Liebknecht, work for reform through parliamentary action. They hope to strengthen their position through a moderate stance. Although they do not reject the idea of revolution, they consider it wrong to push this to the foreground, and they expect more from the one bird already firmly in their hand than the two in the bush. Quite distinct from these more practical social

democrats, however, are the theoretical social democrats such as Schaeffle. They do nothing else than design a plan for erecting a new society and they abstain strictly from anything that smells of agitation and violence. The label "collectivist" hails from these theoreticians and really belongs only to them. See M. Schönberg, *Die Ziele und Bestrebungen der Sozial-demokratie*, 10th ed. (Leipzig: Levien, 1890).

84. *Ed. note*: State socialism was the name given to Bismarck's legislative program of the 1880s to help the German working classes and draw them away from other forms of socialism. The program included health insurance, accident and disability insurance, and old age pensions. Because prominent academics wrote in support of it, it was nicknamed *Katheder-sozialismus*. Their ideal resembles what today we call the welfare state.

85. This school emerged from conservative quarters in Germany, so is native to that country. In his book *Le socialisme d'Etat* (Paris: Calmann Lévy, 1890) Léon Say gives a neat description of this state socialism—to warn the French against it! It is the antipode to social democracy in that it is imposed from the top down. Nevertheless, from its standpoint it has been a strong advocate for the common people, and Rudolf Meyer contributed not a little to the rise of the socialist movement through his book *Der Emancipationskampf des vierten Standes in Deutschland*, 2 vols. (Berlin: Aug. Schindler, 1874–75). State socialism has also given rise to the Christian school of Todt and Stöcker. Emile de Laveleye is not exactly what one might call a state socialist, but his position in fact follows the same line. Adolph Wagner called his school the "sozialrechtliche" [the social justice school]. He agrees with Schmoller more than other authors. His chief work is his textbook for political economy [*Lehr- und Handbuch der politischen Oekonomie*], of which three volumes have come out thus far: vol. 1: *Grundlegung*, 2nd ed. (Leipzig: C. F. Winter, 1879); vol. 5: *Finanzwissenschaft*, 3rd ed. (Leipzig: C. F. Winter, 1884); and vol. 6: *Fortsetzung* (Leipzig: C. F. Winter, 1880). He supports Stöcker.

86. The Historical School is a broader name for the so-called *Kathedersozialisten*, a term of contempt that Oppenheim gave them. Gustav von Schmoller, Erwin Nasse, Lujo Brentano, and M. Schönberg were the founders of this group, which bears close affinity with state socialism. Their system is especially directed against the Manchester school, and to the extent that it aims more at historical studies it is creating a following and finding support also

outside Germany's borders, that is, in Letourneau, *L'Evolution de la propriété*; Alfred Fouillée, *Propriété sociale et la démocratie* (Paris: Hachette, 1884); and others.

87. The radicals on the one hand come close to state socialism, on the other to *Katheder* socialism, at times so close that the boundary line is erased. Their group, also in our country, is not yet organized as a school—hence their differences about state involvement or private initiative are not visible all that much. That the liberals are also moving over to the left is less the result of conviction than of the desire to stay on top by means of timely concessions. Still, the socialistic trend of our age is too powerful also for them to be ashamed of the name "socialist." Even Naquet exclaims: "I for my part am profoundly socialist"; see his *Socialisme collectiviste et socialisme libéral*, 202. And Frédéric Passy, in his lecture of April 9, 1890, about the "Ecole de la liberté," is no more inclined to waive the honor of the label "socialist."

88. The same pantheism that wipes out all differences in the moral domain and dares to place Nero next to Jesus as an equally intriguing contemporary, also leads in the sociological domain to the most shallow and cynical fatalism. The situation is wretched, concludes the pessimist, but there is no way to improve it. We slide down the incline until we sink into the abyss. All this is our destiny. And then perhaps, on the ruins of our civilization a wholly new building program can commence. *Perhaps?* But these pessimists know nothing of the enduring dynamism that lies hidden in the heart of the Christian nations and that can therefore rise above that which spelled ruin for Babylon, Athens, and Rome.

89. It is the age-old problem of the one and the many that recurs here. The starting point of both social democrats and liberals is individualistic, the individual person, and hence Pelagian free will. That the dynamic of the French Revolution is also operating in the social democrats is clear from their continually recurring demand that adult male individuals should rule the affairs of state and society by majority vote. They do not even *understand* our demand that the starting point should be the family.

90. *Ed. note*: In a prayer at the congress, Kuyper had prayed: "They cannot wait, not a day, not an hour."

91. *Ed. note*: In this northern province, desperate farmhands walked off the job. They staged mass demonstrations and compiled blacklists of farmers who hired those willing to work.

92. Bilderdijk, letter no. clxi in *Briefwisseling met Tydeman*, 2 vols. (Sneek: Van Druten & Bleeker, 1866–67), 2:76–83, expressed himself in very strong terms:

> There is nothing for it but to restore civil society to its original purpose. If there is land, let men cultivate it. If there is shipping or fishing, let men expand it. If these three are not enough, organize factories and see to it that everyone can find work for his hands and arms and so provide bread for himself with a wife and children. Oblige all to work and install free and compulsory industry, free and compulsory agriculture. Attach honor to free and shame to compulsory labor. Let no one who steps forward be without honest labor, and have no tolerance for begging. Land, shipping, fishery, and industry—these will support the working classes. No more is needed. Whoever aims to profit from this arrangement is driven by a wrong spirit. If money is lacking at the start, it will be a duty to raise the funds, just as it is for national defense; *frustra armis tuemur, quos fame necamus* ["It is vain to protect with weapons those whom we kill through starvation"]. *Prospicere subditis* ["Looking after subjects"] includes, besides protection against foreign and domestic violence, also the *subsidia vitae* ["life's necessities"] and the *promotio subolis perpetua, quâ non tantum conservetur sed et augeatur res publica* ["constant promotion of offspring which not only preserves but also increases the state"].
>
> There you have in broad outline what every country should make the primary duty. What matters is not to deliberate how to get rid of the poor or prevent their increase, but to make them well-off through work and have them increase in chastity and godliness. He who does not know this does not know how to govern; he who does not want this is an enemy of mankind (whether he means well, according to his lights, or not).
>
> It is true that this becomes more difficult to the extent that perverse commerce has made money more common and so made life's necessities more expensive, which at the slightest recession increases poverty and spreads want, creating incalculable misery. But where there is a will there is a solution. For it is not the quantity of money but its circulation that creates wealth and produces enough surplus.

And in a more general sense he writes:

> Only, all is tainted because money has been made the end-all and be-all instead of a mere means of exchange. As long as this persists the misery will continue and become rampant. This is the great plague that has gone out over Europe, and only those who have the seal of God on their forehead and rest in His providence are immune to it and refuse to work or beg for money but despise it. These few do suffer; yet God will feed them.

He is no less harsh against high finance and the service of Mamon: "All the nations of Europe serve this Mammon, and their only recovery lies in overthrowing the false system. The case is irrefutable. *No bread* for those who are willing to work clashes with the basic law of all work: 'In the sweat of thy face shalt thou eat bread.'"

93. This follows from the creation and the curse. God himself created us with such a nature that we are subject to metabolism: our bodies need food, which is then consumed so that we must eat again. Likewise, the curse, on account of sin, has made it necessary both to clothe our bodies out of shame and to shield them against the cold.

94. The words in John 12:8, "For the poor you always have with you," do not establish a *rule* but state a *fact*; they do not say that it ought to be so, but at most that it will always prove to be so. Secondly, it will not do to conclude from a concrete saying about that period that Jesus was at the same time prophesying about *later centuries.* And in the third place, this totally overlooks the reproach hidden in these words. The Greek here does not have *meth' humoon* but *meth' heautoon*, that is, you will always have the poor in the social circle you are forming. This was said to Judas and his ilk—people who carry the money bag and handle it the way Judas did.

I hope this comment clarifies my saying "God forgive them." As for the very tolerable condition of the poor in Israel, see the fine rectorial address by my worthy colleague D. P. D. Fabius, *Mozaïsch en Romeinsch recht* (Amsterdam: J. A. Wormser, 1890), 69ff. On the same page a footnote also explains the statement in Deuteronomy 15:11, "For there will never cease to be poor in the land." [*Ed. note*: Paul Fabius taught law at the Free University of Amsterdam. He was an exacting and meticulous scholar, and his political sympathies were decidedly conservative; during the preparation for the congress he had angrily accused Kuyper of doing no more than taking his cue from the socialists.]

95. This point cannot be emphasized enough. We too, for our part, ought to be engaged in study and action. We will not make any progress in tackling the social question with sentimental talk or shallow generalities. That was the mistake of the earlier communists and utopian dreamers like Fourier and Proudhon. Socialism is a power to be reckoned with precisely because of its studies and serious research. To be convinced of this, go through the historical surveys of Quack, Winterer, Villard, and others; or, better yet, the systematic studies of Deville, Block, and Blondel. Of Gabriel Deville I recommend his work *Le Capital de Karl Marx.* Even more extensive is Maurice Block, *Les progrès de la science économique depuis Adam Smith,* 2 vols. (Paris: Guillaumin, 1890); it comes in two volumes and is rich in citations. And a work without a historical survey but providing a summary of the history in the course of expounding its own system is *La question sociale et sa solution scientifique* (Paris: Guillaumin, 1887), by Jules Edouard Blondel. It is therefore most desirable that the law faculty of the Free University furnish us with advice on this score.

    To see the difference between the old and the new research method, compare Wilhelm Roscher's *Geschichte der National-Oeconomik in Deutschland* with Johann Joseph Rossbach's *Geschichte der Gesellschaft,* 8 vols. (Wurzburg: Stuber, 1868–75).

96. This point is paramount in the whole social question. If I do not reckon with God I am entirely free in reconstructing society and can make it as I please. Man then becomes the maker of society in the strictest sense of the word, and he will violate natural laws wherever they stand in the way or push aside the moral law whenever it forms an obstacle. However, if the starting point is belief in God, who created both our human nature and the nature around us and gave laws for both, then all human social action is bound to the ordinances of God in nature and in the moral law as taught by Scripture.

97. Denying this duality leads either to state absolutism and state deification, or to anarchy. No third possibility exists. You cannot have a constitutional state unless the duality of government and people is recognized and the relation between the two is regulated in law. The capital error of our constitution, which gives half of legislative power to parliament, is on that account so very questionable. All monism on this point leads to pantheism. The theism

of the Christian religion demands the duality and therefore the contrast between the people as subject to God and the government as servant of God—the institution to which God has entrusted the care of the people.

98. On the atomistic standpoint the entire gospel would collapse. For then there would be no incarnation of the Word, no Head of the church, no original sin, and therefore no atonement through the blood of the cross. It would be a fatal uprooting of all Christian certainty, beginning with a denial of original sin and solidarity in guilt, followed by a denial of the glorious doctrine of the covenants. This is the very reason why Christians must firmly defend the organic and therefore the social character of human life. This comes to expression in a most moving way in the commandment to love one another. See Adolf Jäger, *Die soziale Frage im Licht der Offenbarung*, 2 vols. (Neu-Ruppin: Rud. Betrenz., 1891); Hans Lassen Martensen, *Socialismus und Christenthum*, trans. from the Danish (Gotha: Rudolf Besser, 1875); Rienzi (pseud. of Henri Hubert van Kol), *Christendom en socialisme* (The Hague: Rh. W. Raadgeep, 1882); and, though presented somewhat oddly, Paul von Lilienfeld, *Gedanken über die Socialwissenschaft der Zukunft*, 4 vols. (Hamburg: E. Behre, 1873–79), 2:403ff.

99. Revolution and history stand only partially opposed to each other. After all, next to the regular process of history there is just as much the disruption of this process through violence. The only defense against revolution as a principle and as a fact is the apostolic word: "Submit yourselves to the higher powers" [see Rom 13:1; 1 Pet 2:13] understood according to the Calvinist interpretation that this passivity finds its limit only in the command to obey God's Word. To be sure, according to the *secret* counsel of God, mutiny and insurrection have their place in history as divine judgments; but God's *revealed* will does not sanction disobedience except for God's sake, and even then never otherwise than as passive resistance. Our forefathers therefore always insisted that the Dutch Revolt against Spain was not a revolt of the people but a legitimate defense of defenseless people by the *magistratus inferiores* [the lower magistrates]. See Voetius, *Catechisatie over den Heidelbergschen Catechismus*, ed. Poudroyen (Dordt, 1662), 636ff., where this question is clearly explained in the spirit of our forefathers in short questions and answers.

100. This is clear from Acts 5:4, where Peter says: "While it remained unsold, did it not remain your own? And after it was sold, was it

not at your disposal?" This shows, first, that Ananias owned still more land; second, that to sell it was not mandatory; third, that giving or not giving the money after selling it remained his free choice. Neither Calvin nor any Reformed exegete understood what we read in Acts 3:44–45 as describing a "community of goods." The only thing that can be inferred from these verses is: (1) that the wealthier brothers sold a considerable portion of their property in order to distribute a portion of the proceeds to the poorer brothers; and (2) that the deacons' chest in the days of the apostles was still so full that no one suffered want.

101. It is imperative that Christians come to realize that the absolute definition of property right, which the French Revolution and its associated economic theory have pushed to extremes, is not necessarily the correct one at all. That realization is best acquired by tracing historically how property has been defined in constantly changing ways throughout the ages and among all peoples. To that end we recommend the work by Letourneau, *L'Evolution de la propriété*, a thorough study that offers an ethnological and chronological survey of the way property has been regulated among different peoples and in different centuries. Once you are convinced through this historical survey that our concept of property is hardly the only one, nor the most attractive one, take this concept, which stems from Roman law, and place it next to the concept of property in Scripture—that God alone is owner because he alone is Creator, and that we are stewards of his goods—and instantly you have a concept of property to work with that is non-socialistic and yet sociological.

The words from the parable: "Am I not allowed to do what I choose with what belongs to me? (Matt 20:15) do not in any way indicate a Christian theory of property right. They simply occur as a detail in a parable, taken from life as it was then. Merely think of the parable of the unjust steward [Luke 16:1–12]. Moreover, this concerns only the right *to give away* what one owns. See P. Poulin, *Religion et socialisme* (Paris: Lacroix, Verboeckhoven, et Co., 1867), 210ff.

102. In my address at the congress I could not say more [about land nationalization, an idea floated by the leadership of Patrimonium in Friesland]. That would have preempted discussion. Hence I confined myself to the general comment that use of the soil cannot fall under the common law of property. This is evident from the distinctive nature of the soil, which is not the product of man's work and is merely worked upon by man. It is also evident from

the special legislation about the land that God gave Israel—by which I do not suggest that we should at once adopt laws that were laid down for Israel, but only that God has lifted this characteristic feature beyond the reach of our criticism. After all, even more strictly than in the case of goods, God himself is Owner of the soil (see Fabius, *Mozaïsch en Romeinsch recht*, 25). To be sure, it does not follow from this that our salvation lies in land nationalization, nor that Mr. Van Houten's idea must become law. But whoever haughtily mocks all such proposals and ideas and brands them as "socialist" is guilty of superficiality and skepticism. Agrarian legislation will always be difficult. Just think of Ireland. Yet that is where the Salisbury Ministry has not honored the sacrosanct nature of land ownership. Compare Henry George's work of 1879, *Progress and Poverty*, cited above. In addition, see J. Stoffel, *De oplossing der sociale kwestie door opheffing van het privaat grondbezit* (Deventer: A. W. Hovenaar Rutering, 1889); Dr. Homo, *De nationalisatie van den bodem* (Haarlem: Met & Meylink, 1883); H. George, *Sociale vraagstukken*, trans. J. Stoffel (Deventer: W. Hulscher, 1884); A. von Miaskowski, *Das Problem der Grundbesitzvertheilung in Entwicklung* (Leipzig: Duncker & Humblot, 1890); and H. von Wendel, *Die landwirthschaftliche Ankaufs- und Verkaufs-Genossenschaften* (Berlin: Parey, 1886). And for a new essay aimed at solving the social question, see O. Effertz, *Arbeit und Boden: Grundlinien einer Ponophysiocratie* (Berlin: Puttkammer & Mühlbrecht, 1889), ix, who adopts the idea of Petby that "Arbeit ist der Vater, die Erde die Mutter der Güter, das Gut ist also als Kind des Vaters Arbeit und der Mutter Erde an zu sehen." ["Labor is the father and soil the mother of goods, hence goods are to be viewed as the children of father Labor and mother Earth."]

103. Scripture gives us not only ideas but also specific ordinances. Christians who say that they bow to God's Word yet in their social and political exertions march with the men of the French Revolution live a double life: they are of two minds and show that they do not understand Scripture and the power of the Word.

104. See his *Briefwisseling met Tydeman*, 2:77.

105. Emigration and colonization cannot be recommended enough, since even though Malthus' law that population grows at a geometric rate while the food supply only at an arithmetic rate has in the meantime proven false—see his *Essay on the Principle of Population*, 7th ed. (London: Reeves and Turner, 1872); and Charles Knowlton,

An Essay on the Population Question (Rotterdam: Van Der Hoeven & Buys, 1878); and the opposite view in Henry George, *Poverty and Progress*—that still does not erase the fact, now that hygiene has considerably lengthened life expectancy, that the population is increasing far too rapidly for the land now under cultivation; its limitation can only be found in a lower birth rate or in mass starvation. That the solution is not the adoption of a two-child system is demonstrated in France; see Franz Mehring, *Social Reform und Ueberbevölkerung*, quoted in Otto Zacharias, *Die Bevölkerungs-Frage in ihrer Beziehung zu den sociale Nothständen der Gegenwart*, 4th ed. (Jena: Mauke, 1883), 36, who is likewise opposed to the two-child system and all physical means [of contraception], yet holds a brief for "moral restraint."

This painful, thorny question cannot be settled with a simple appeal to the words "Be fruitful" unless one also adds "and fill the earth." Colonization must therefore be made more prominent. Of the 1,434 million people who inhabit the earth today, 1,000 million live on one seventh of its surface. That leaves six sevenths for only 434 million people, that is, 3 or 4 souls per square kilometer. Even after subtracting glaciers, deserts, and steppes there remain 56 million square kilometers, that is, a region as large as all Asia, which could provide abundant food for hundreds of millions of people. See Wilhelm Votsch, *Die Vertheilung der Menschen über die Erde* (Berlin: Habel, 1884), 44.

106. The means suggested by the advocates of the two-child system have promoted prostitution to an unbelievable degree, and it is an outrage that in our enlightened age these means of sin are openly recommended in the major newspapers of the leading centers of culture. But even apart from this issue, the social question is to a high degree a moral question. The service of Mamon turns into the service of Ashtoreth. A woman's honor is for sale for money, and poverty then encourages putting oneself up for sale. See Louis Martineau, *La prostitution clandestine* (Paris: Delahaye, 1885); Louis Reuss, *La prostitution au point de vue de l'hygiène* (Paris: J.-B. Baillière, 1889); Emile Richard, *La prostitution à Paris* (Paris: J.-B. Baillière, 1890); plus the many publications elicited in our country by the strong initiatives of H. Pierson. [*Ed. note*: Rev. Hendrik Pierson (1834–1923) was the director of an asylum for ex-prostitutes, a home for unwed mothers, and an orphanage. He played a leading role in the European movement to abolish the legalization of prostitution.]

107. For this reason, and this reason alone, we must oppose tuition-free schools, school meals, school showers, and so on. It is one thing to wonder whether parents who have no money should not be given money to help them take care of their children. But the state should never take child-rearing away from the parents. That weakens our national strength.

108. Bathing in sweat, but then also eating bread.

109. Work too is a divine ordinance, one that is governed in the first place by the question how we are to view the worker. And then the answer is clear: we are to view the worker as a human being, created in the image of God, sin-ridden, destined for an eternal existence, and here on earth called to take his stand in society as a husband and a father, to share with us the ups and downs of sickness and health, youth, maturity, and old age. Cardinal Newman and Pope Leo XIII rightly agree with this, and Mr. Van Houten's critique may show that these facts by themselves cannot solve the question yet in no way does he prove that ours is not the right starting point. We may not be at peace with the social order until it offers to all men an existence worthy of human beings. Until such time it will remain a target of our critique. Only, do not expect a solution from monetary help from the state. That will always be humiliating for a person's sense of self-worth as well as debilitating for our national strength. The help the state must offer is better legislation. Even the various brands of socialism only half recognize this; see F. J. Haun, *Das Recht auf Arbeit* (Berlin: Puttkammer & Mühlbrecht, 1889); Edmond Guillard, *Protection et organisation du travail* (Paris: Guillaumin, 1887); James E. Thorold Rogers, *Work and Wages* (London: Swan Sonnenschein, 1890), 154ff.; David Ricardo, *Rente, salaires et profits* (Paris: Guillaumin, 1888); N. G. Pierson, *Grondbeginselen der staathuishoudkunde*, 3rd ed. (Haarlem: Bohn, 1891), 109; Conrad Bornhak, *Die deutsche Sozialgesetzgebung* (Freiburg: Mohr, 1890), 9; and Falckenberg in his fine dissertation of 1891 [*Ed. Note*: This is perhaps a reference to Paul Falkenberg, *Der Eigentumserwerb von dem veräußernden Nichteigentümer nach Handelsrecht* (Diss.: Univ. Leipzig, 1891)]. See also the introduction in L. Smith, *Les coalitions et les grèves* (Paris: Guillaumin, 1885), and the important discussion about "weekly rest from the social point of view" at the international congress held in Paris under the chairmanship of Léon Say; see *Congrès international du repos hebdomadaire* (Paris: Guillaumin and Fischbacher, 1890).

In the labor question, too, the atomistic approach corrupts everything: work by the hour and by the man-hour, when in fact two organic ties govern work: first, that of the work to be rendered (think of field work as compared to work in a large factory); and second, that of the life cycle of the workingman (youth, manly strength, old age, illness, and health).

110. See my *Eenige Kameradviezen uit de jaren 1874 en 1875* [Selected speeches in parliament from the years 1874 and 1875] (Amsterdam: J. A. Wormser, 1890), 191–97. [*Ed. note*: The actual date of the cited speech was Nov. 28, 1874.]

111. Our Antirevolutionary Party, too, must take care not to be carried along by state socialism. Even though we stand directly opposed to the individualism of the Liberal party, we nevertheless subscribe wholeheartedly to the warning given by Goshen, which Léon Say, *Le socialisme d'Etat*, 214, translates thus: "If we have learned anything from history, we could say that the self-confidence of the individual and the respect of the state for natural liberty are necessary conditions for statehood, the prosperity of society, and the greatness of a people." The whole Antirevolutionary program is set up along these lines. It would indeed be safest to concentrate all our strength on the organization of labor and labor contracts.

112. Nothing enriches our Christian working classes so much as strict abstinence from strong drink. With the money thus saved thanks to self-control, they enjoy better food and God places a double blessing on their meager portion. That blessing results especially from the fact that they do not allow their desires to be stimulated by false stimulants. After all, where such stimulants are at work one is never satisfied and therefore never happy. This can be seen in high-income families that still complain loudly and never know the peace of having their needs satisfied. Desire always asks for more, and to stimulate desire is to arouse dissatisfaction and so spoil happiness.

113. How offensive, when churches distinguish between gentlemen and burghers, and burghers and the poor, preferably with a separate "chapel" for the poorest members. It becomes even more offensive when during the Lord's Supper the gentlemen do not want to sit next to the workmen, and when in regions where ear irons are still worn, the ladies with the golden irons go first, to be followed by the women with the silver ones. Such practices are pagan. Christ wants us have affection for each other as *brothers and sisters*.

114. It is perfectly true that if no help is forthcoming from elsewhere, the state must help. We are not allowed to let anyone die of hunger so long as bread still lies molding in so many breadboxes. Also, when the state helps it must do so quickly and adequately. (An indictment of our poor law!) But for that very reason it deserves emphasis that public relief is and remains, not our badge of honor, but a stinging indictment of the church and the rich—the consequence of a liberalism that undermined the strength of the church and made the rich egotistical.

115. *Ed. note*: Reference to the delegates from the Christian Workingmen's Federation that cosponsored the congress. The other sponsor was the Antirevolutionary Party, which Patrimonium had accused of favoring the middle and upper classes and never nominating one of their own in a winnable district. The congress was organized in part to head off the formation of a Christian labor party.

116. I speak of "restoring" trust because at the most recent annual meeting of Patrimonium it became apparent that this had been undermined. There was a reason for this. Workingmen cannot devote time to studies, and the men among us whose duty it is to make the social question a topic of concentrated study from a Christian perspective have thus far woefully fallen short in fulfilling this duty. The lower class feels this, and that feeling breeds mistrust.

117. He who does not believe in the power of the Christian religion to lift society out of a condition not unlike bankruptcy, can only conclude with P. Jacoby, *Etude sur la sélection* (Paris: Baillière, 1881), 535, that the civilized nations of today are destined to sink into barbarism and to be succeeded by younger nations that are still in an underdeveloped state. See Letourneau, *L'Evolution de la propriété*, 495. See also especially the excellent work by James Fitzjames Stephens, *Liberty, Equality, Fraternity* (London: Smith, Elder & Co., 1873).

118. I have deliberately included in these notes references to some interesting titles in order to be of service perhaps to those among us who are still complete strangers to this field.

For Further Reading

Papal Social Letters in the Line of *Rerum Novarum*

Leo XIII. Encyclical Letter on Capital and Labor, *Rerum Novarum* (May 15, 1891).

Pius XI. Encyclical Letter on Reconstruction of the Social Order, *Quadragesimo Anno* (May 15, 1931).

John XXIII. Encyclical Letter on Social Progress, *Mater et Magistra* (May 15, 1961).

John XXIII. Encyclical Letter on Establishing Universal Peace, *Pacem in Terris* (April 11, 1963).

Paul VI. Encyclical Letter on the Development of Peoples, *Populorum Progresso* (March 26, 1967).

Paul VI. Apostolic Letter on the Occasion of the Eightieth Anniversary of the Encyclical *Rerum Novarum*, *Octogesima Adveniens* (May 14, 1971).

John Paul II. Encyclical Letter on Human Work, *Laborem Exercens* (September 14, 1981).

John Paul II. Encyclical Letter on the Social Concern of the Church, *Sollicitudo Rei Socialis* (December 30, 1987).

John Paul II. Encyclical Letter on the Hundredth Anniversary of *Rerum Novarum*, *Centesimus Annus* (May 1, 1991).

Benedict XVI. Encyclical Letter on Integral Human Development, *Caritas in Veritate* (June 29, 2009).

Francis. Encyclical Letter on Our Common Home, *Laudato Si'* (May 24, 2015).

Selected Papal and Vatican Documents

Pius XII. Address *Radio Message for the 50th Anniversary of* Rerum Novarum (June 1, 1941).

Vatican Council II. Pastoral Constitution on the Church in the Modern World, *Gaudium et Spes* (December 7, 1965).

John Paul II. Encyclical Letter on the Value and Inviolability of Human Life, *Evangelium Vitae* (March 25, 1995).

Catechism of the Catholic Church. Second Edition. Washington, DC: United States Conference of Catholic Bishops, 2000.

Pontifical Council for Justice and Peace. *The Social Agenda: A Collection of Magisterial Texts.* Edited by Robert A. Sirico and Maciej Zieba. Vatican City: Libreria Editrice Vaticana, 2000.

Pontifical Council for Justice and Peace. *Compendium of the Social Doctrine of the Church.* Vatican City: Libreria Editrice Vaticana, 2004.

Benedict XVI. Encyclical Letter on Christian Love, *Deus Caritas Est* (December 25, 2005).

Francis. Apostolic Exhortation on the Proclamation of the Gospel in Today's World, *Evangelii Gaudium* (November 24, 2013).

Additional Bibliography

Anderson, Clifford B., and Kenneth Woodrow Hale. "Meeting Together for the Good of the World: Christian Social Congresses Tried to Transform the Economic Order." *Christian History*, no. 104 (2013): 29–32.

Bacote, Vincent. *The Spirit in Public Theology: Appropriating the Legacy of Abraham Kuyper.* Eugene, OR: Wipf & Stock, 2010.

Ballor, Jordan J. "The Church's Social Witness and the Further Work of the Reformation." *Journal of Christian Legal Thought* 5, no. 2 (Fall 2015): 11–16.

———. "The Moral Challenges of Economic Equality and Diversity." *Philosophia Reformata* 78, no. 2 (2013): 196–208.

———. "A Society of Mutual Aid: Natural Law and Subsidiarity in Early Modern Reformed Perspective." In *Law and Religion: The Legal Teachings of the Catholic and Protestant Reformations*, edited by Jordan J. Ballor, Wim Decock, Michael Germann, and Laurent Waelkens, 9–21. Göttingen: Vandenhoeck & Ruprecht, 2014.

————. "State, Church, and the Reformational Roots of Subsidiarity." In *The Myth of the Reformation*, edited by Peter Opitz, 148–59. Göttingen: Vandenhoeck & Ruprecht, 2013.

Ballor, Jordan J., ed. "Modern Christian Social Thought." Theme Issue. *Journal of Markets & Morality* 14, no. 2 (Fall 2011).

Ballor, Jordan J., and Robert Joustra, eds. *The Church's Social Responsibility: Reflections on Evangelicalism and Social Justice.* Grand Rapids: Christian's Library Press, 2015.

Ballor, Jordan J., Peter Heslam, and Manfred Spieker, eds. "Integral Human Development." Theme Issue. *Journal of Markets & Morality* 16, no. 1 (Spring 2013).

Barry, John S. "On the Universal Destination of Material Goods," *Religion & Liberty* 10, no. 1 (January/February 2000): 5–7.

Bavinck, Herman. "General Biblical Principles and the Relevance of Concrete Mosaic Law for the Social Question Today (1891)." *Journal of Markets & Morality* 10, no. 2 (Fall 2010): 437–46.

Beabout, Gregory R. "The Principle of Subsidiarity and Freedom in the Family, Church, Market, and Government." *Journal of Markets & Morality* 1, no. 2 (October 1998): 130–41.

Bishop, Steve, and John H. Kok, eds. *On Kuyper: A Collection of Readings on the Life, Work & Legacy of Abraham Kuyper.* Sioux Center, IA: Dordt College Press, 2013.

Bliss, William D. P., ed. *The Encyclopedia of Social Reform.* New York: Funk & Wagnalls, 1897.

Bolt, John. "Abraham Kuyper and the Holland-America Line of Liberty." *Journal of Markets & Morality* 1, no. 1 (Spring 1998): 35–59.

————. "Calvinism, Catholicism, and the American Experiment: What is the Question?" *Journal of Markets & Morality* 5, no. 1 (Spring 2002): 183–92.

————. *A Free Church, a Holy Nation: Abraham Kuyper's American Public Theology.* Grand Rapids: Eerdmans, 2001.

————. "Herman Bavinck's Contribution to Christian Social Consciousness." *Journal of Markets & Morality* 13, no. 2 (Fall 2010): 413–36.

Bratt, James D. *Abraham Kuyper: Modern Calvinist, Christian Democrat.* Grand Rapids: Eerdmans, 2013.

————. "Adding Context to Text and Theory." *Faith & Economics* 67 (Spring 2016): 105–11.

————. "Passionate About the Poor: The Social Attitudes of Abraham Kuyper." *Journal of Markets & Morality* 5, no. 1 (Spring 2002): 35–44.

————. "Sphere Sovereignty among Abraham Kuyper's Other Political Theories." In *The Kuyper Center Review: Volume 1, Politics, Religion, and Sphere Sovereignty,* edited by Gordon Graham, 34–49. Grand Rapids: Eerdmans, 2010.

Bratt, James D., ed. *Abraham Kuyper: A Centennial Reader.* Grand Rapids: Eerdmans, 1998.

Browning, Don S. "Religion and Civil Society: In James Luther Adams, Abraham Kuyper, and Catholic Social Teachings." *Criterion* 47, no. 3 (2010): 14–25.

Bruijn, Jan de. *Abraham Kuyper: A Pictorial Biography.* Translated by Dagmare Houniet. Grand Rapids: Eerdmans, 2014.

Bruijne, Ad de. "'Colony of Heaven': Abraham Kuyper's Ecclesiology in the Twenty-First Century." *Journal of Markets & Morality* 17, no. 2 (Fall 2014): 445–90.

Burton, Katherine. *Leo XIII: The First Modern Pope.* New York: D. McKay, 1962.

Calvez, Jean-Yves, and Jacques Perrin. *The Church and Social Justice: The Social Teaching of the Popes from Leo XIII to Pius XII, 1878–1958.* Chicago: Regnery, 1961.

Chaplin, Jonathan. "Subsidiarity as a Political Norm." In *Political Theory and Christian Vision: Essays in Memory of Bernard Zylstra,* edited by Jonathan Chaplin and Paul Marshall, 81–100. Lanham, MD: University Press of America, 1994.

————. "Subsidiarity and Sphere Sovereignty: Catholic and Reformed Conceptions of the Role of the State." In *Things Old and New: Catholic Social Teaching Revisited,* edited by Francis P. McHugh and Samuel M. Natale, 175–202. Lanham, MD: University Press of America, 1993.

————. "Subsidiarity: The Concept and the Connections." *Ethical Perspectives* 4 (1997): 117–30.

Colson, Charles W. "How Now Shall We Live?" *Journal of Markets & Morality* 5, no. 1 (Spring 2002): 287–304.

Coppa, Francis J. *The Modern Papacy since 1789.* New York: Routledge, 2013.

Donati, Pierpaolo. "What Does 'Subsidiarity' Mean? The Relational Perspective." *Journal of Markets & Morality* 12, no. 2 (Fall 2009): 211–43.

Dulles, Avery Cardinal. "Religious Freedom and Pluralism." *Journal of Markets & Morality* 5, no. 1 (Spring 2002): 169–82.

Eglinton, James, and George Harinck, eds. *Neo-Calvinism and the French Revolution.* New York: T&T Clark, 2014.

Fremantle, Anne, ed. *The Papal Encyclicals in Their Historical Context.* New York: Mentor Books, 1956.

Gilson, Étienne, ed. *The Church Speaks to the Modern World: The Social Teachings of Leo XIII.* New York: Image Books, 1954.

Goudzwaard, Bob. "A Response to Michael Novak's 'Human Dignity, Personal Liberty.'" *Journal of Markets & Morality* 5, no. 1 (Spring 2002): 113–25.

Giertych, Wojciech. "*Rerum Novarum* in the Light of *Libertas.*" *Journal of Markets & Morality* 19, no. 2 (Fall 2016).

Grasso, Kenneth L., and Robert P. Hunt, eds. *Catholicism and Religious Freedom: Contemporary Reflections on Vatican II's Declaration on Religious Liberty.* Lanham, MD: Rowman & Littlefield, 2006.

Hall, David W. "A Response to Johan D. van der Vyver's 'The Jurisprudential Legacy of Abraham Kuyper and Leo XIII.'" *Journal of Markets & Morality* 5, no. 1 (Spring 2002): 251–75.

Harinck, George. "A Historian's Comment on the Use of Abraham Kuyper's Idea of Sphere Sovereignty." *Journal of Markets & Morality* 5, no. 1 (Spring 2002): 277–84.

———. "Neo-Calvinism and the Welfare State." In *The Kuyper Center Review: Volume 1, Politics, Religion, and Sphere Sovereignty,* edited by Gordon Graham, 93–105. Grand Rapids: Eerdmans, 2010.

Harinck, George, and Lodewijk Winkeler. "Sphere Sovereignty (1870–1914)." In *Handbook of Dutch Church History,* edited by Herman J. Selderhuis, 487–520. Göttingen: Vandenhoeck & Ruprecht, 2015.

Heslam, Peter S. *Creating a Christian Worldview: Abraham Kuyper's "Lectures on Calvinism."* Grand Rapids Eerdmans, 1998.

———. "Prophet of a Third Way: The Shape of Kuyper's Socio-Political Vision." *Journal of Markets & Morality* 5, no. 1 (Spring 2002): 11–33.

Himes, Kenneth R., ed. *Modern Catholic Social Teaching: Commentaries & Interpretations.* Washington, DC: Georgetown University Press, 2005.

Hochschild, Joshua P. "The Principle of Subsidiarity and the Agrarian Ideal." In *Faith, Morality, and Civil Society*, edited by Dale McConkey and Peter Augustine Lawler, 37–64. Lanham, MD: Lexington, 2003.

Kennedy, James C. "The Problem of Kuyper's Legacy: The Crisis of the Anti-Revolutionary Party in Post-War Holland." *Journal of Markets & Morality* 5, no. 1 (Spring 2002): 45–56.

Koyzis, David T. "Differentiated Responsibility and the Challenge of Religious Diversity." *Journal of Markets & Morality* 5, no. 1 (Spring 2002): 199–207.

Kuipers, Tjitze, ed. *Abraham Kuyper: An Annotated Bibliography 1857–2010*. Leiden: Brill, 2011.

Kuyper, Abraham. "Christ and the Needy (1895)." *Journal of Markets & Morality* 14, no. 2 (Fall 2011): 647–83.

———. "Commentary on the Heidelberg Catechism Lord's Day 42 (1895)." *Journal of Markets & Morality* 16, no. 2 (Fall 2013): 713–57.

Lee, Hak Joon. "From Onto-theology to Covenant: A Reconstruction of Abraham Kuyper's Sphere Sovereignty." In *Public Theology for a Global Society: Essays in Honor of Max L. Stackhouse*, edited by Deirdre King Hainsworth and Scott R. Paeth, 87–102. Grand Rapids: Eerdmans, 2010.

Luckey, William R. "Catholic Reflections on the Basis of the Pluralist Structure of Society." *Journal of Markets & Morality* 5, no. 1 (Spring 2002): 95–111.

Lugo, Luis, ed. *Religion, Pluralism, and Public Life: Abraham Kuyper's Legacy for the Twenty-First Century*. Grand Rapids: Eerdmans, 2000.

McIlroy, David H. "Subsidiarity and Sphere Sovereignty: Christian Reflections on the Size, Shape, and Scope of Government." *Journal of Church and State* 45, no 4. (Autumn 2003): 739–63.

Mouw, Richard J. *Abraham Kuyper: A Short and Personal Introduction*. Grand Rapids: Eerdmans, 2011.

———. *The Challenges of Cultural Discipleship: Essays in the Line of Abraham Kuyper*. Grand Rapids: Eerdmans, 2012.

———. "Law, Covenant, and Moral Commonalities: Some Neo-Calvinist Explorations." In *Public Theology for a Global Society: Essays in Honor of Max L. Stackhouse*, edited by Deirdre King Hainsworth and Scott R. Paeth, 103–20. Grand Rapids: Eerdmans, 2010.

Mueller, Franz H. "The Principle of Subsidiarity in the Christian Tradition." *American Catholic Sociological Review* 4 (1943): 144–57.

Noll, Mark A. "A Century of Christian Social Thought." *Journal of Markets & Morality* 5, no. 1 (Spring 2002): 137–56.

Novak, Michael. "Human Dignity, Personal Liberty: Themes from Abraham Kuyper and Leo XIII." *Journal of Markets & Morality* 5, no. 1 (Spring 2002): 59–85.

Pahman, Dylan. "Toward a Kuyperian Political Economy: On the Relationship between Ethics and Economics." *Faith & Economics* 67 (Spring 2016): 57–84.

Rey, Dominique. "The Meaning of *Rerum Novarum* for Western Europe Today." *Journal of Markets & Morality* 19, no. 2 (Fall 2016).

Roels, Shirley, ed. "Common Grace in Business." Theme Issue. *Journal of Markets & Morality* 18, no. 1 (Spring 2015).

Röpke, Wilhelm. "Liberalism and Christianity." Translated by Patrick M. Boarman. *Modern Age* 1, no. 2 (Fall 1957): 128–34.

Schindler, Jeanne Heffernan, ed. *Christianity and Civil Society: Catholic and Neo-Calvinist Perspectives.* Lanham, MD: Lexington, 2008.

Schmiesing, Kevin. "Brothers and Sisters of Charity: A Catholic Response to a Transformed World." *Christian History*, no. 104 (2013): 15–20.

Schmiesing, Kevin, ed. *One and Indivisible: The Relationship between Religious and Economic Freedom.* Grand Rapids: Acton Institute, 2016.

Skillen, James, and Rockne McCarthy, eds. *Political Order and the Plural Structure of Society.* Atlanta: Scholars Press, 1991.

Spieker, Manfred. "Development of the Whole Man and of All Men: Guidelines of the Catholic Church for Societal Development." *Journal of Markets & Morality* 13, no. 2 (Fall 2010): 263–78.

———. "Freedom and its Limits, 1891–2015: How Does Catholic Social Doctrine React to New Challenges?" *Journal of Markets & Morality* 19, no. 2 (Fall 2016).

———. "The Universal Destination of Goods: The Ethics of Property in the Theory of a Christian Society." *Journal of Markets & Morality* 8, no. 2 (Fall 2005): 333–54.

Stockwell, Clinton. "Abraham Kuyper and Welfare Reform: A Reformed Political Perspective." *Pro Rege* 27, no. 1 (1998): 1–15.

Stout, Jeffrey, "Christianity and the Class Struggle." In *The Kuyper Center Review: Volume 4, Calvinism and Democracy*, edited by John Bowlin, 40–53. Grand Rapids: Eerdmans, 2014.

VanDrunen, David. "The Importance of the Penultimate: Reformed Social Thought and the Contemporary Critiques of the Liberal Society." *Journal of Markets & Morality* 9, no. 2 (Fall 2006): 219–49.

Van Dyke, Harry. "How Abraham Kuyper Became a Christian Democrat." *Calvin Theological Journal* 33, no. 2 (November 1998): 420–35.

Van Leeuwen, Mary Stewart. "Faith, Feminism, and the Family in an Age of Globalization." In *Religion and the Powers of the Common Life*, vol. 1, *God and Globalization*, edited by Max L. Stackhouse with Peter J. Paris, 184–230. New York: T&T Clark, 2000.

Van Til, Kent A. "Subsidiarity and Sphere-Sovereignty: A Match Made in...?" *Theological Studies* 69, no. 4 (2008): 610–36.

Vyver, Johan D. van der. "The Jurisprudential Legacy of Abraham Kuyper and Leo XIII." *Journal of Markets & Morality* 5, no. 1 (Spring 2002): 211–49.

Waterman, A. M. C. "*Rerum Novarum* and Economic Thought." *Faith & Economics* 67 (Spring 2016): 29–56.

Weigel, George, and Robert Royal, eds. *A Century of Catholic Social Thought: Essays on* Rerum Novarum *and Nine Other Key Documents*. Washington, DC: Ethics and Public Policy Center, 1991.

Weinberger, Lael Daniel. "The Relationship between Sphere-Sovereignty and Subsidiarity." In *Global Perspectives on Subsidiarity*, edited by Michelle Evans and Augusto Zimmermann, 49–64. Dordrecht: Springer, 2014.

Witte, John, Jr., and Frank S. Alexander, eds. *The Teachings of Modern Christianity on Law, Politics, and Human Nature*. New York: Columbia University Press, 2006.

Wolfe, Christopher. "Subsidiarity: The 'Other' Ground of Limited Government." In *Catholicism, Liberalism, and Communitarianism: The Catholic Intellectual Tradition and the Moral Foundations of Democracy*, edited by Kenneth L. Grasso, Gerard V. Bradley, and Robert P. Hunt, 81–96. Lanham, MD: Rowman & Littlefield, 1995.

Wolterstorff, Nicholas. "A Response to Michael Novak's 'Human Dignity, Personal Liberty.'" *Journal of Markets & Morality* 5, no. 1 (Spring 2002): 87–93.

Woude, Rolf van der. "Taming the Beast: The Long and Hard Road to the Christian Social Conference of 1952." *Journal of Markets & Morality* 14, no. 2 (Fall 2011): 419–44.

Zieba, Maciej. *Papal Economics: The Catholic Church on Democratic Capitalism, from* Rerum Novarum *to* Caritas in Veritate. Wilmington, DE: ISI, 2013.

About the Contributors

Pope Leo XIII (born Vincenzo Pecci, 1810–1903) enjoyed the Roman Catholic Church's third longest pontificate. Prior to his election as pope in 1878, he served as provincial administrator in Benevento and as bishop of Perugia. His many encyclicals on social, political, and economic issues reflect his vast experience and knowledge of matters related to church, state, and society.

Abraham Kuyper (1837–1920) was a leading Dutch figure in education, politics, and theology. He was a pastor, was elected to parliament, and served as prime minister of the Netherlands from 1901 to 1905. In addition to writing on a wide array of theological, political, and social topics, Kuyper also founded the Free University (VU) in Amsterdam, a political party, and a denomination.

Jordan J. Ballor (Dr. theol., University of Zurich; Ph.D., Calvin Theological Seminary) is a senior research fellow and director of publishing at the Acton Institute for the Study of Religion & Liberty, where he also serves as executive editor of the *Journal of Markets & Morality*. He is author and editor of numerous volumes, and a general editor of Sources in Early Modern Economics, Ethics, and Law and Abraham Kuyper Collected Works in Public Theology.